The Thrifty Cookbook

The Thrifty Cookbook

476 ways to eat well with leftovers

Kate Colquhoun

illustrations by Will Webb

BLOOMSBURY

LONDON · BERLIN · NEW YORK

First published in Great Britain 2009

Copyright © 2009 by Kate Colquhoun
Illustrations copyright © 2009 by Will Webb

The moral right of the author has been asserted.

Bloomsbury Publishing Plc, 36 Soho Square, London W1D 3QY

Bloomsbury Publishing, London, New York and Berlin

A CIP catalogue record for this book is available from the British Library.

ISBN 978 0 7475 9704 9
10 9 8 7 6 5 4 3 2 1

Printed and bound in Italy by Grafica Veneta S.p.A.

This book is printed on 100% recycled paper called 'Editor 2',
which is made without the use of chlorine or optical brighteners.
'Editor 2' obtained the 'Ecolabel' trademark that is the recognition
that the European Union grants to 'Friends of the Environment'
products manufactured with low energy consumption and
minimum air and water pollution.

www.bloomsbury.com
www.thethriftycook.co.uk

Note: No food was wasted in the writing or production of this book.

What's Thrifty Cooking?

Cooking with food that you might otherwise simply throw out makes sense in all sorts of ways. Creating something tasty from languishing fruit or vegetables, extending the life of fresh meat by using marinades, preserving gluts in jams or chutneys, or simply using up a bowlful of leftover meat, rice or pasta will not only save you money but also make a substantial environmental difference.

This kind of thrifty cooking is not about making an impression. Most of the time it's more likely to be throwing something together quickly for lunch or an evening in front of the telly or with a good book. It's about being relaxed without compromising on quality and taste, the kind of cooking that you simply can't be fetishistic about. This is not the place for purism or marvellous presentation. So that's a relief.

I don't think many of us realise how much food we throw away, but the statistics are astonishing: 6.7 million tonnes a year and rising. That's a third of all the food we buy, and enough to fill Wembley stadium to the brim eight times a year. Half of it is meat bones, teabags, eggshells and vegetable peelings but the other half could be eaten. To put things in perspective, our domestic waste is three times more than the total waste from supermarkets. Which is not to say that the food industry and the public sector don't have their own backyard to clear up – the food chain is still generating 11 million tonnes of waste – but it does put much of the responsibility for change back on our own doorstep.

We live in a world where half of us are killing ourselves with excess calories while the other half starve, in a society that spends more on dieting than on food aid and where health and safety legislation means that it is criminal to donate perfectly viable food that's reached its use-by date to the homeless. And though we might get into a lather about the environmental sustainability of food miles or the ethics of battery chickens, the amount of food we send to landfill each year is the skeleton in the cupboard. It's only alarming when the bin bag breaks, disgorging its slimy contents all over the floor; the rest of the time we don't notice.

There is, of course, a significant environmental cost to all this. In landfill sites, rotting food, airless in its black bags and compressed by the weight bearing down on it, creates methane – a greenhouse gas 23 times more powerful than carbon dioxide – and a poisonous black sludge that seeps into our watercourses. Around 20 per cent of our greenhouse gas emissions are associated with food production, distribution and storage. It's estimated that if we just stopped wasting food, we could reduce our carbon dioxide equivalent emissions by at least 15 million tonnes a year – the same as taking one in every five cars off the road. This is far more than we could ever achieve by cutting out food packaging or the use of plastic bags. Amazing.

Closer to home, food waste costs hard-earned cash. UK households are binning around 15 pence in every food pound: something like £15,000–24,000 in a lifetime and worth around £10 billion a year, which is more than the UK's foreign aid budget. Around £2.3 billion of that is food chucked out in its original packaging, and that includes 5,500 chickens and 1.2 million sausages *a day*. Add to that almost 4.5 million apples and only slightly fewer potatoes every day, plus around 328,000 tonnes of bread a year – figures that are both staggering and depressing.

Food is cheap – we spend a lower proportion of our income on it than at any time in our history – so no wonder we value it less and are easily seduced into buying too much of it at once. But food prices are on the rise, driving inflation as fast as oil and gas prices. As unpredictable weather patterns cause crop failures, we're already noticing the food bills more. Global wheat prices doubled and rice prices trebled during 2007, while eggs are up almost 60 per cent and pasta over 110 per cent. That's going to start to hurt.

Unlike most of our Continental neighbours or families in Asia and the Middle East, who still use up their food with imagination and without embarrassment to make two, four or even more meals, we've broadly lost the knack – perhaps the first generation to give up on taking leftovers and food past its best seriously. But returning to traditions of buying less, wasting less and honouring food and its production more shouldn't be difficult. Price rises will feel a little less burdensome if you know you're going to get several good meals out of what you buy, refusing – like granny – to waste a scrap.

It's not so much about boring frugality as about making food that tastes really good – think of Italy, where leftover dishes such as Ribollita,

Arancini and Bread Salad or 'Panzanella' (see pages 60, 140 and 213) are some of the finest in the repertoire. There's no need to rehash the same old meat endlessly throughout the week any more than to collect the lard for greasing cartwheels. Actually, it *is* worth having lard around because there are times when it tastes better and works better than olive oil: roast potatoes are a case in point. But you don't have to buy it – you can save the fat from a roast. Stock cubes and bouillon powders are fine, but there's something really *good* as well as useful about a simple home-made stock. And it's virtually free. Long after it's lost its right to live on the breadboard, the last bit of bread can be used in puddings, salads or soups, or kept in the freezer as breadcrumbs to use in meatballs or as the crunchy top of a bake, zesty with lemon and pungent with garlic and herbs.

Cooking with leftovers in delicious, imaginative and easy ways and using up raw food that would otherwise be thrown away is a vital part of the continuum for anyone who cares about their food. I have to say that much of what follows in this book might seem like stating the bleeding obvious – that fresh herbs and good spices are essential components of making food tasty; that one simple extra ingredient from a store cupboard or picked up on the way home can transform all the bits in the fridge that need to be used up; that meat that's already been cooked is not going to give up any more juices; that you can do different things with leftovers depending on how much you have to work with. But bear with me. This kind of cooking is also, often, about inverting the normal scheme of things. Instead of being seduced by a new recipe and then rushing out to get the ingredients, you'll be looking at what you have to hand and then deciding what kind of taste and texture you want and what kind of cooking you're in the mood for: a soup, pie or stir-fry, a salad, stew or bake? Sometimes – as with meat in stir-fries – the method will completely reverse the usual way of doing things and, except when you are making pastry or baking cakes, precise measures are not going to matter.

In some ways, recipes themselves are suspect, because this is all about practicality and imagination. Most of these recipes work on rough amounts – a British teacupful (about 175ml) of meat per person, say, for a pie – and they describe basic processes that can be endlessly varied, with lots of ideas on how you can change things about. Meat, for example, can be omitted from almost any recipe and replaced with vegetables that are crying out to be used up. To help get you started, I've included a basic list of the kind of flavours that go together well (see pages 26–7). The knack is to taste and taste again as you cook, altering the combinations of herbs and seasonings and developing the recipe ideas in the pages that follow to suit your own style.

Thrifty cooking is not about bland and colourless dinners for the sake of saving a chicken wing. With fresh cream in just about every corner shop, olive oil on every shelf and inspiration flooding in from all corners of the globe, there need be nothing plain about this food – nothing stopping it from being as good (or better) than it was the first time around. I bet most of us have got the Christmas leftover thing taped through sheer force of practice, and this book is really just an extension of that. With a bit of planning, a thoughtful array of cupboard staples, judicious use of space in the freezer and experimentation with what goes with what, using up food properly can become something of an addictive habit. The last carrots in the fridge can be transformed into a curried pickle that will enliven a basic pilaf, a couple of blackened bananas make a lush banana cake, while a lingering single egg white is easily whisked into a meringue that will keep in a tin for weeks, if you've got that kind of self-control. Taking these recipes as a guide, you can eke out several good meals from one big roast – conjuring 'free' food out of what, yesterday, you might have considered rubbish.

These are ideas you can play with, alter and refine according to your own taste; they are quick and unfussy, requiring very little preparation and producing even less washing up. Using up food you might otherwise chuck means you are doing your bit for sustainability, and it should leave you with more cash in your pocket, more space in your fridge and a welcome reconnection with your kitchen. Cheap to the point of being free, it's not just about common sense – it is tasty and infinitely, almost smugly, rewarding. And, yes, it could even help change your world.

How to Waste Less Food

Once you start to notice how much food gets thrown away, it's amazing how your mindset alters – what used to be unconsciously acceptable becomes irritating. Becoming aware of waste almost immediately begins to change the way you shop, store and plan to use your food. So what follows is really only plain common sense.

Shopping

The single best way to cut down on food waste is to make a shopping list and stick to it. My granny had a plastic board with a wax pencil dangling on the end of a thrillingly scarlet ribbon – now I use it. My mum used to write with a washable black felt-tip pen on the white ceramic tiles above her workspace. I loved the element of graffiti that entered her normally well-ordered kitchen.

I tell myself that being methodical about food shopping doesn't make me a fuddy duddy. It's nicer to think that it makes me savvy, streetwise and environmentally responsible and it does save on endless excursions to the shops to get one extra ingredient. If you stick to the list and generally refuse to be seduced, it should mean that you have what you need (and just what you need) in the fridge and cupboard, rather than an odd array of all your favourite foods that don't quite go together.

Lists also save money. Supermarkets have long been experts at making us buy more than we need and we are endlessly optimistic about how healthy we *might* be – stocking up on too much perishable food. Then there's the fact that pre-packed fruit, vegetables and meat are rarely exactly the right amount, so that some of it goes mouldy before it's even been touched. Seductive Buy One, Get One Free offers (delightfully known as BOGOFS) might be good value for pasta or shampoos, if you can remember where you've stored them, but with fresh food they more often simply fuel our increasingly throwaway culture.

Buying less, more often and, if possible, locally means that if you suddenly find you are having a particularly sociable week and are hardly at home, you are not left with a load of food rapidly demanding attention. It makes buying cheaper seasonal foods easier, cuts out the toil of a once-a-week marathon shop, is likely to reduce packaging and – believe it or not – is often significantly cheaper. Shopping locally is not just about supporting your local community in the battle against supermarket supremacy; it is almost guaranteed to reduce your overall food bill as well.

If you regularly throw away, say, one pear at the end of every week, then stop buying the four-packs and go for three single pears bought locally instead. Put yourself back in charge of how many, what size and what degree of ripeness you want, with the added advantage that you will be reducing packaging too. You could also consider getting your weekly (or monthly) basics delivered by an online supermarket, freeing you up to buy fresh produce as needed. I reckon the average urban family can save around £100–200 a month shopping like this.

Your Basic Stores

Think of the kitchen as having three storage areas – the cupboard, the fridge and the freezer. Getting them under control may mean a little investment up front but is ultimately less wasteful. A can of beans or pulses can turn leftover meat into a tantalising soup, stew or salad, while coconut milk and curry paste mean you won't be phoning out for a delivery of curry and chucking some leftovers in the bin. Bottled ingredients such as capers and anchovies last for ages in the fridge and will perk up almost any dish instantly. And I don't want to live in a world without frozen pastry – it turns something boring into something glorious.

If the following list looks daunting, I am not suggesting that you rush out and buy everything at once, and you certainly don't need everything on it to make the most of these recipes. The list is general, and you probably have most of it already. There might be a couple of ingredients here that you haven't used before but in small quantities none of them is expensive. The point is: build up what you need and ignore the rest.

Packets

- Pasta: penne, lasagne, linguine, spaghetti, Chinese egg or rice noodles
- Rice: short grain risotto rice (such as Arborio, Carnaroli or Nano), long grain rice (such as basmati)
- Couscous
- Lentils (dry or canned) – green, Puy or red
- Bouquet garni or bay leaves
- Stock powder – unlike most stock cubes, Marigold vegetable bouillon has no preservatives, artificial flavours or GM ingredients
- Flour: plain, self-raising; strong white flour for pizzas
- Sugar: caster; soft brown or muscovado
- Coleman's English mustard powder
- Nuts: pine nuts, walnuts, almonds
- Seeds: fennel, sesame, coriander, cumin, pumpkin, caraway
- Dried fruit: raisins, sultanas, apricots, dates
- Spices: dried chilli flakes, nutmeg, saffron stamens, cardamom pods, paprika; a good curry powder or ground cumin and garam masala; dried (or frozen) kaffir lime leaves
- Dried mushrooms: porcini/cep
- Salt and pepper

Cans, bottles, etc.

- Canned plum tomatoes
- Canned beans: flageolet, cannellini, borlotti, butterbeans, chickpeas
- Coconut milk
- Bottled anchovy fillets
- Bottled mini gherkins (cornichons)
- Bottled capers
- Bottled artichoke hearts
- Tuna: I prefer 'dolphin friendly', and fish packed in oil rather than brine
- Oil: a good extra virgin olive oil for salads, ordinary olive oil for everyday; sunflower or vegetable oil for deep-frying; tasty oils such as sesame for stir-fries and walnut for salads
- Vinegar: white or red wine, cider, malt (for chutneys) and the best aged balsamic you can afford – the thicker and more syrupy (without the addition of molasses) the better

- Vermouth or Martini – the end of a bottle of dry white wine will also usually do the trick
- Mustard: wholegrain and smooth French mustard
- Thai curry pastes (red or green)
- Sauces: soy, Worcestershire, Tabasco, Thai fish sauce (also called *nam pla*)
- Honey, preferably runny
- Vanilla extract

Fruit and veg basics
- Onions: red, white, shallot, spring – up to you
- Garlic
- Carrots
- Potatoes
- Lemons and oranges

Fridge basics
- A tube or jar of tomato purée
- Bacon: streaky or back, smoked or not
- Cheese: Cheddar and Parmesan
- Butter
- Eggs
- Crème fraîche or double cream, plain yogurt

Freezer basics
- Peas
- Broad beans
- Bacon – with a very sharp knife you can trim off what you need from the frozen block
- North Atlantic prawns
- Pastry: shortcrust and puff
- Woody herbs, chopped parsley
- Breadcrumbs
- Bread: most breads freeze well; bagels and pitta bread are especially useful
- Leftover wine (really!) for use in cooking

Food Labels

We used to use our senses to help make decisions about whether to cook or chuck, but food labels can be pernicious, encouraging us to abandon our own judgement in favour of remote estimation. So here's the thing: if food is clearly rotten and unsalvageable, it will have to be thrown out or composted. If it smells odd, if it's turned a funny colour, has mould on it or is slimy, then bin it. Heat will intensify the smell of rotten food, so if that piece of slightly iffy bacon starts to throw off an intense, gamy smell once it's under the grill or in the pan, it probably shouldn't be there in the first place. Bottom line – if in any doubt, chuck it out.

Most raw meat, however, is perfectly fine for consumption even if it has just slipped over its label date: touch it, look at it closely and above all smell it. Bread may become stale but it's fine to eat, preferably toasted, as long as there are no mould spots. Likewise, the mouldy bits can be cut off cheese or fruit, leaving the good parts for eating – they are often bursting with the best flavour as they reach the end of their lives. You should never take chances, but you *can* trust yourself to make your own careful decisions.

The reality behind food labelling is this:

Best-before dates

This refers to quality rather than food safety and most food is fine to eat beyond these dates, though the taste and texture may not be at their very best. This also applies to canned, dried and frozen food.

Government advice is that eggs should not be eaten after the best-before date, though I admit I do it sometimes. You just *know* when an egg is off – it rattles, for a start, and once cracked open it stinks. If in doubt, put a whole egg into a bowl of water: fresh eggs will sink and rotten eggs float; anything in between is suspect. In this case, crack the egg into a separate bowl and smell it before adding it to anything else; if it doesn't smell, it's fine to use.

Keep refrigerated

Best before	Use by	Weight
22-DEC	24-DEC	70g e

Use-by dates

These are meant to indicate when food should absolutely not be eaten beyond a certain period. Government advice on this is unequivocal.

But you can still use your common sense if the use-by date was yesterday. Food approaching its use-by date can be frozen to extend its viable life. Once defrosted, it should be eaten immediately.

Sell-by dates

These are instructions for shop staff, not cooks, designed simply to help with stock control.

Storing Food

It's obvious that the better food is wrapped and stored, the longer it will last: think of the difference between a piece of well-wrapped, juicy Cheddar and the bit that dried out when it fell out of its packet. So any kitchen needs a few plastic boxes in different sizes for the fridge and freezer. Special bags are also handy, but you can equally use old take-away containers, empty ice-cream or yogurt pots, or even empty plastic bottles for soups, sauces and stocks. Keep even the really tiny pots that used to hold something delicious and unnecessary and use them to store an unused handful of grated cheese or an egg yolk. It's finicky, but the truth is that they hold *just enough* to use in something like lunchtime soup, and once you get into the habit of not chucking food, it's hard to go back. If you've had one too many mornings tearing your hair out as you try to find the right box and lid for a packed lunch, stack the boxes by size and store the lids in an empty, square ice-cream tub – the smallest lids will still try to hide, but they have less space in which to be imaginative.

You'll also need cling film to cover bowls in the fridge and foil for wrapping leftover joints of meat.

The Store Cupboard

If you are anything like me, you sort through the cupboard from time to time and find cans, spice jars and half-used packets well past their best-before date. Some end up in the bin; the rest go back to fight another day.

No one is so perfectly controlled that they are going to get it right all the time, and spices can be particularly difficult. All I can suggest is that you buy the small packets, that you don't have too many and that you keep them in some sort of order. It's better, anyway, to buy small amounts of whole spices than ready-ground ones: they keep longer, and grinding them just before you use them means that the taste stays fresh.

In some respects, the less storage space you have, the easier your life will be. I have one store cupboard, just big enough to hold packet or canned basics, plus a minute cupboard under the stairs for storing reserves. When the spaghetti in the store cupboard runs out, I hope there will be a backup under the stairs. Then back to the shopping list on the fridge to make a note to replace it. Lack of space frees me from the tyranny of storing goods in date order: nice idea, if you have that kind of discipline.

Apart from the cupboard, I use an old metal bread bin for storing root vegetables. Once in the dark and cool, they last several weeks – always take off the plastic wrapping or they will start to sprout.

The Fridge

When you read about our ancestors' struggles to keep food fresh, you have to be grateful to the inventor of the electric fridge. The downside is that we are now so used to bunging stuff into it that much comes back out again only to go straight into the bin. Some of that problem will simply disappear if you buy smaller amounts more often, though with the best will in the world there will always be a wilting courgette lurking somewhere that will need a quick fix.

The five basic rules for fridges are:
- They should be set at 5°C – salmonella grows at 7°C.
- Cooked food should be cool before you store it in the fridge.

- Raw and cooked food should be kept on separate shelves.
- If you over fill the fridge, it becomes inefficient – so buy less, more often.
- All leftover food stored in the fridge should be well covered, wrapped in cling film or stored in an airtight box.

Things to bear in mind...

Cooked meat Keeps in the fridge for a good 3–5 days. Cover it while it cools, then put it straight into the fridge, well wrapped, or sliced and tightly packed in an airtight box to stop the slices drying out.

Stuffings Should always be removed from the meat, as they cool more slowly and provide an ideal breeding ground for bacteria. Keep them separately in a covered bowl or box and use them in stews or soups for extra flavour and thickening.

Cooked vegetables Will keep in the fridge for 3–5 days.

Dips Will last 3–5 days in the fridge, if kept airtight.

Fresh cream Keeps 5–7 days once opened, depending on the date on the carton; whipped cream keeps 1–2 days only.

Raw eggs Keep 2–4 days.

Fish Raw fish keeps 1–2 days; cooked fish 3–4 days.

Minced meat Keeps 2–3 days.

Bacon Keeps 7–10 days.

Joints or cuts of red meat Keep 3–5 days, raw or cooked.

Poultry, whole or joints Keeps 3–5 days, raw or cooked.

Sausages Keep 3–5 days, raw or cooked.

The Freezer

Like cupboards, a relatively small freezer is easier to maintain than a cavernous chest into which the peas from some long-gone era have sunk like the *Titanic*. Just one word of caution: don't freeze leftover food that you didn't like first time around. It will sit there for months and end up being chucked out anyway, doubling the guilt.

On the other hand, one of the best ways to save time and money in the long run is to plan to make larger quantities than you know you will need for one meal, just so you can freeze some of it for later: waste-free ready meals, if you like, that will be at hand for when you just can't face cooking or when your children's friends descend unexpectedly – cheaper and tastier than anything you could buy. Stews freeze wonderfully in small amounts, as do soups, casseroles and bakes. Meatballs, lasagne, fish pie, cottage and shepherd's pies and moussaka are all stalwart freezer fodder.

Whatever you freeze, wrap it well – freezer 'burn' dries out and toughens some foods, particularly meat, and it happens when the food is not tightly wrapped in cling film, foil or a bag. Remember, too, that liquid expands as it freezes, so don't overfill containers, especially with soups and sauces.

If you have ever wondered what all those stars mean, here's the low-down:

* (-6°C): suitable for ice cubes or to store food for 3–4 days
** (-12°C): store food for 2–3 weeks
*** (-18°C): store food for 1–3 months
**** (below -18°C): for rapid freezing and to store food for 3–12 months

Most of us know that frozen food will, in fact, last for longer than is officially recommended – a year even – though its quality won't be great. But that seems like a waste of effort and space to me. The thing to remember is that *freezing will not kill bacteria already present in the food*, so eat it as soon as possible after defrosting.

All sorts of things that might otherwise be thrown away can be frozen, making quick suppers really easy:

Leftover meat Cut into smallish dice and pack in an airtight box or bag for future use in risottos, pies, soups or stir-fries; it will keep for a good couple of months.

Leftover cream, wine, gravy or stock The last tablespoon of cream at the bottom of the carton, the half glass of wine left in the bottle, even the last small jug of gravy, can be frozen. If you have the patience, pour them into an ice-cube tray and then decant the frozen cubes into freezer bags so you can use them as you like.

Breadcrumbs These are useful for so many different meals that it's worth keeping a largish airtight box of them, regularly adding the ends of stale (but not mouldy) pieces of bread. Thirty seconds or so in the food processor is all it takes. It means that there might be an unholy mix of white and brown, fine and slightly coarser crumbs at any one time in the same container, but I don't find that disconcerting. They will keep indefinitely in the freezer (or for 2–3 weeks in the fridge).

Herbs Woody herbs like thyme and rosemary keep really well in a plastic ziplock bag in the freezer if you don't feel like hanging them up to dry. Softer herbs fare less well, though parsley is fine if it is finely

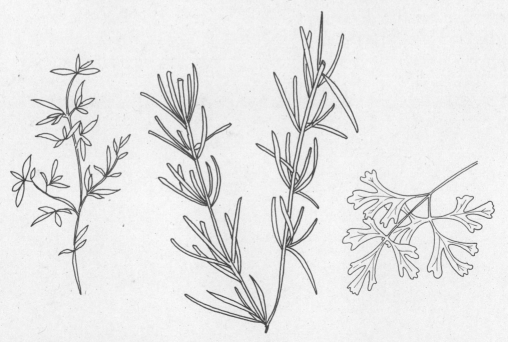

chopped while fresh and then frozen on a baking tray before being tipped into a box – use it for soups and stews straight from frozen. Basil does not freeze well but lemongrass does: after defrosting, bruise it well with a rolling pin and remove the woody outer bark before use. I also keep fresh ginger root in the freezer, which makes it very easy to grate, producing a lemon-coloured mound of fine Parmesan-like snow.

Whole tomatoes Remove the stalks; the tomatoes will be mushy once defrosted but are fine to use in sauces, soups and stews.

Fruit I keep a bag of frozen berries in the freezer for emergency puddings.

Egg yolks Can be frozen but they do go very sticky and can be hard to use. It's usually better to store them in a covered bowl in the fridge for up to 4 days, or turn them into Custard (see page 33), Zabaglione (page 200) or Hollandaise Sauce (page 35) for a spoiling weekend breakfast of eggs Benedict.

Egg whites Can be frozen in a small bag or box (with a label saying how many there are).

The best way to defrost food is to stick it on a plate and put it in the fridge to thaw out slowly. Remember to cook it soon after it has defrosted – and don't re-freeze it simply because you have changed your plans. You can, however, make it into soups, stews and so on and then refreeze it.

If you are in a rush, you can speed up the defrosting process by immersing frozen food in cold water in the sink. Make sure that it is tightly wrapped in a bag or box or you'll end up with a watery mess. Change the water every 30 minutes or so to keep the process moving. Microwaves are also useful for defrosting but, because they can leave warm spots in the food, which are perfect breeding grounds for bacteria, you should then cook the food immediately.

How Much to Cook

The dreary words 'portion control' trail a distinct whiff of uninspired caterers and airline food. But bear with me here – getting the amounts you cook just a bit more accurate will save money as well as landfill.

Pasta and rice in particular just never quite look *enough* in their raw state and I almost always cook too much. Most of us do, actually. They're relatively cheap, and we're so used to doing it that we hardly notice. We throw away an enormous amount of pasta – around 87,000 tonnes a year.

There are broad guidelines for what the average adult will eat, though the reality is that you do need different amounts according to what you're cooking: a stew, for instance, needs far more meat than a stir-fry, while a risotto will use more rice than you would need for a side dish. I reluctantly began to weigh ingredients before cooking them (particularly pasta and rice) when I started to get my knickers in a twist about food waste. At first I found it rather trying but, judging by the fact that I now have far fewer bowls of leftovers in the fridge, it works.

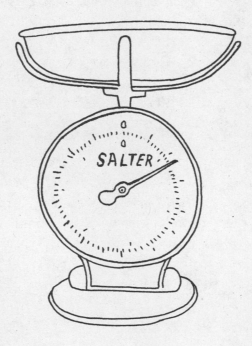

Here, then, are some very general measures that you can use as a rule of thumb:

Pasta 100g per adult, around 60g for a primary-school-age child.

Rice 80g per adult, 50g per child (or about 2½ tablespoons per child).

Mashed potato About 200g per adult, 100g per child (peeled weight of raw potatoes).

Vegetables The recommended single-portion amount for a five-a-day diet is 80g per adult, about 50g for a child. Or you can work to 3 heaped tablespoons per adult, 1–2 for children.

Dried pulses and beans Around 80g or 3 heaped tablespoons per adult, 50g for children.

Meat or fish You'll need more for a stew, less for a pie, but work on the rough basis of around 140g per adult, 100g per child.

Some Basics

To make the most of whatever leftovers you are planning to cook with, you might need to pick up one basic ingredient as you pass the shops – something simple but transformatively 'right'. That's when it helps to have in your head an idea of some perfect partners.

What Goes with What

This is such a big subject that the following ideas really just scrape the surface. But the point about just *knowing* some of this stuff is that it cuts down on the looking-up part of cooking, and it also means that you can pick up a carton of yogurt, a bag of mushrooms, a lemon or a fennel bulb on your way home, knowing that it's the only thing you need besides what's in your store cupboard to turn leftovers into something delicious. Tastes differ, but here are a few bedfellows generally accepted to have kicked along in a pretty ideal way. Add your own ideas to the list as you notice great combinations in restaurants or cookbooks.

Chicken Tarragon, mushrooms, chilli, lemon (both fresh and preserved), olives, garlic, leeks, saffron

Lamb Garlic, mint, anchovy, cumin, aubergines, yogurt, capers, chickpeas, rosemary, preserved lemon, thyme, ginger, red peppers

Beef Chilli, mustard, horseradish, mushrooms, onions, bacon, green beans, tomatoes

Pork Lemon, apples, thyme, juniper, soy sauce, mustard, beans, Puy lentils, fennel, leeks, lemon, bay leaves, vermouth, prunes, celery

Fish Lemon, lime, dill, parsley, lentils, fennel, capers, saffron, leeks, tomatoes, potatoes

Sausages Red cabbage, potatoes, cider, apples, purple broccoli, bay leaves, chickpeas, beans and chilli powder, Puy lentils, peas, leeks, roast peppers

Potatoes Cheese, onions, mint, parsley, chives, bacon, peas

Parsnips Celeriac, sweet potato, carrots, cheese, thyme, rosemary, chilli

Aubergines and courgettes Mint, basil, tomatoes, chilli, garlic

Leeks Cheese, mustard, mushrooms, sage

Peas and broad beans Bacon, lettuce, mint, tarragon, shallots, spring onions

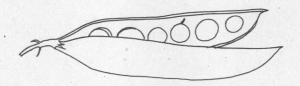

Making Stock

You don't have to make stock. Stock powders or even water are fine for most things but, having grown up in a home where stock was always in the fridge, I can't really imagine living without it. Apart from the cost of energy from the stove, stock is almost entirely free and it means that you've used up *every bit* of the goodness of the food you've bought. It will keep for seven to ten days in the fridge or can be frozen for months; just remember to reheat it to boiling point before use.

As well as making it as described overleaf, you can, by the way, make stock in a covered casserole dish in the oven at 150°C/Gas Mark 2, which saves energy. Alternatively, follow the instructions on your pressure cooker.

Meat Stock

Meat stock can be made from almost any bones – though beef, chicken and ham will probably be the most useful. Use the bones or carcass left over from a roast or, if your butcher bones a piece of meat for you, bring the bones home and roast them first at 200°C/Gas Mark 6 for 40–45 minutes, until they are brown and sticky.

I've also shown below how to clarify meat stock. For hundreds of years, cooks have done this with egg white to produce a shining clear broth – delicious with some freshly cooked noodles, sliced spring onions or a little leftover meat.

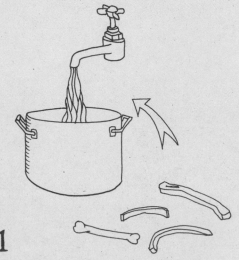

1

To make the stock, put the leftover or separately roasted bones into your largest saucepan and cover with water.

2

Throw in 5 black peppercorns, a bay leaf or bouquet garni, a peeled carrot, half a peeled onion and a celery stalk (if you have a lot of bones, you could double these quantities).

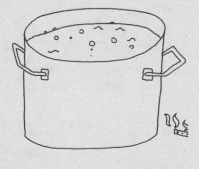

3

Bring slowly to the boil and then simmer very gently, uncovered, for about 2 hours. The stock will be clearer if you skim off the froth from the top with a slotted spoon from time to time.

4

When the stock is ready, strain it. Discard the bones, allow to cool, then refrigerate.

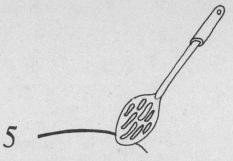

5

If there is any fat, it will rise to the surface and harden. I lift it off with a spoon and throw it out.

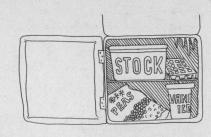

6

Store the stock in a covered bowl or plastic box in the fridge, or freeze in plastic boxes, bowls or soup bags. (To save space, you can boil the stock until reduced by about two-thirds. When you come to use it, just bring it back to its original volume by adding water.)

How to clarify meat stock

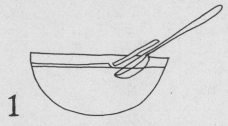

1

Once the stock has been strained and cooled, and any fat on the surface has been removed (see above), return the stock to a clean pan and bring to a slow simmer.

2

In a small bowl, lightly whisk an egg white (for up to 1.5 litres liquid; use 2 egg whites for more liquid).

3

Add this to the simmering stock and swirl with a spoon. The egg will turn white almost immediately. Barely simmer for a couple of minutes and lift the egg out with a slotted spoon, discarding it.

4

Strain the stock through a sieve lined with a square of kitchen paper, then cool and refrigerate, or freeze as usual.

Fish Stock

As with meat stock, you can use the heads and bones left over from whole cooked fish or bring home bones from the fishmonger's if you have asked them to fillet your fish for you (unlike raw meat bones, these do not need roasting before use).

Fish stock is invaluable for use in fish pies, risottos and fish soup. Follow the instructions for Meat Stock on the previous pages, using fish carcasses, heads and tails from white fish (avoid oily fish), or shells from prawns, crabs, lobsters, etc, but simmer the stock for just 20–30 minutes. If you've got any prawn or langoustine shells, toast them first in a frying pan (without oil) before adding them to the stock.

Vegetable Stock

Vegetable stock makes the lightest of broths, and is also ideal for risottos, stews, soups, etc. Follow the instructions for Meat Stock on the previous pages, using either the last few vegetables from the fridge, roughly chopped, or clean vegetable peelings, or even the pods left over from shelling fresh peas or broad beans (but avoid starchy vegetables like potatoes and parsnips). The stock needs to simmer for just 20–30 minutes.

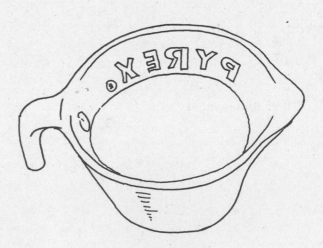

Using Fats

When I was a child, almost all the meat fat was saved as dripping and then used for cooking the Sunday roast of beef or lamb, or for helping the potatoes and other roast vegetables on their way. If you want it to, it can take the place of olive oil in cooking.

If you are roasting a duck or goose, pour off the rivers of melting fat and keep in a covered bowl or jar in the fridge for roasting potatoes; the fat 'boils' at a high temperature, helping to make the crispest roast potatoes possible. Pour the fat from almost any roast meat (except chicken, which will not set) into a small bowl and store in the fridge. Use this 'dripping' whenever you roast another joint or for Yorkshire puddings – times when olive oil just doesn't have the same effect.

I don't, by the way, keep the fat from frying bacon, as its taste is almost too powerful to use with anything else. But I do keep all the bacon rinds until I have a good handful and bake them in a moderate oven (180°C/Gas Mark 4) until they have turned into a crispy bird's nest. Better than crisps. Please *don't* pour any fats down the sink. Let them cool and then put them in a sealed plastic bag in the bin – or invest in a biodegradable fat trap (see page 248), designed to be kept in the fridge until it's full and then thrown away.

Easy Sauces

Sauces are crucial for leftovers: home-made mayonnaise will transform post-Christmas sandwiches, while a good hollandaise turns the ends of boiled ham into a perfect eggs Benedict with the help of a toasted muffin and a poached egg. A good white, cheese or tomato sauce can form the basis of a bake, gratin or stew and all of them compensate for the fact that leftover meat is more likely to be dry than juicy. Then there's custard, an ideal way of using up egg yolks and a perfect accompaniment to fruit, whether stewed, baked or in pies or crumbles. It's worth getting the hang of these basic sauces – many of the recipes in this book refer back to them.

White Sauce

White sauce, or béchamel, comes in handy for fish pie, moussaka, cauliflower cheese and other vegetable bakes, pies and soufflés. If you warm the milk before you start, it makes things much easier.

30g butter
30g plain flour
400ml warm milk (or half single cream and
*   half milk, if you want a richer sauce)*
freshly grated nutmeg
salt and pepper

Melt the butter in a small pan over a very low heat without letting it colour. Stir in the flour and cook for 30 seconds or so. Very gradually pour in the warm milk, using a small whisk or wooden spoon quite actively to prevent lumps forming. As it starts to simmer, the sauce will thicken – keep adding more milk, a little at a time, whisking as you go. If lumps do begin to form at the start of the process, let the sauce bubble back into a thick but sloppy paste before adding the milk again, whisking all the time.

When all the milk has been added, let the sauce cook, with hardly a bubble, for 5 minutes or so, until thick, smooth and creamy. Season with salt and pepper – and a grating of nutmeg, if you like (especially good with lasagne).

Cheese Sauce

Make the White Sauce above, adding 2 good handfuls of grated Parmesan, Cheddar or other fairly strong hard cheese when it is cooked. The cheese should melt even when the heat is turned off. Taste it as you go, adding more or less cheese according to taste. A level teaspoon of your favourite mustard will add spike.

Custard

Custard is a great way of using up egg yolks. You may not be aware that, unless it makes a fanfare about it, bought custard rarely contains any egg at all. Make it if you are planning a meringue fest, as a way of using up all the unwanted egg yolks – or you can make it anyway and freeze the whites (see page 22).

With custard, you need to watch the heat: too much, too fast, and the mixture might scramble or separate. So go easy, using a non-stick pan and a wooden spoon for stirring.

Serves 4

3 egg yolks
1 tablespoon caster sugar
275ml single cream – or milk, if you prefer

Whisk the yolks and sugar together in a good-sized bowl. Bring the cream or milk *just* to boiling point. Pour this slowly over the egg and sugar mixture, whisking constantly as you do so. Now pour the lot into a clean, heavy-based saucepan, turn the heat very low and stir the custard gently but constantly with a wooden spoon until it begins to thicken. By thicken I don't mean *thick* – it should coat the back of the spoon without dribbling right off, and that's all. Remove from the heat and strain through a sieve.

If, despite all your best efforts, the custard does start to curdle, pour it into a clean bowl, put this in the sink, and let cold water come half way up the side of the bowl. Whisk vigorously. This works around 50 per cent of the time and there is almost nothing you can do with curdled custard if it doesn't.

The very end of a jug of home-made custard This can be baked in a little ramekin at 180°C/Gas Mark 4, preferably in a small roasting tin containing enough water to come half way up the side of the ramekin. Add a few berries, if you like, or a topping of soft brown sugar, and bake for 10–15 minutes, until set. Allow to cool, then set aside for a solitary lunchtime pudding.

Mayonnaise

Hellmann's is great, but fresh mayonnaise has its particular appeal and making it really isn't complicated. You can pep it up with all sorts of chopped ingredients – garlic, herbs, cornichons, anchovies, capers and the like – to go with steak, fish, salads or sandwiches. Think of a tarragon mayo with cold chicken, dill mayo with cold salmon or caper mayo with cold boiled ham. As any Belgian knows, garlic mayonnaise is pure luxury with chips or spooned over boiled potatoes.

I use a food processor, which is easier, though you can do it by hand in a bowl with a whisk or wooden spoon. Go slow with your pouring hand.

The quantities below make a generous amount for sandwiches and salads; the mayonnaise will keep in the fridge, covered, for 3 days.

2 large egg yolks
1 teaspoon mustard (English or Dijon)
1 teaspoon white wine vinegar
a pinch of salt (unless you are adding
    anchovies, gherkins or capers)
250ml basic olive or groundnut oil
    (in other words, oil without a strong taste)
black pepper

Whiz together the egg yolks, mustard, vinegar and salt in a food processor. With the machine running, pour in the oil in a very slow, steady stream (if you are making the mayonnaise by hand you will need to add it, almost literally, drop by drop). Pour too fast and the oil and egg will separate. What you want is for them to emulsify into a fairly thick, creamy sauce. Taste and adjust the seasoning.

If by chance the mayonnaise does separate, take a clean bowl and whisk another egg yolk in it. Then add the separated mixture a drop at a time, whisking vigorously as you go. It should all come back together.

Hollandaise Sauce

Hollandaise is very similar to mayonnaise but you make it in two stages
to produce a more robust sauce that is served tepid – a perfect partner
for artichokes, spinach, poached eggs and leftover fish or fishcakes.
Rich with egg yolks, this sauce will curdle if it is over-heated. If this
happens, turn down the heat and make sure the hot water in the pan is
not touching the bottom of the bowl. Whisk a single egg yolk in a cup
and add it slowly to the original mixture, whisking all the time – with
luck, it should come back together again.

Hollandaise will keep in the fridge, covered, for 3 days.

Serves 4 generously

2 tablespoons white wine vinegar
3 tablespoons water
a squeeze of lemon juice
1 small shallot, very finely chopped
5 black peppercorns
3 large egg yolks
175g unsalted butter, diced
salt and pepper

Put the vinegar, water, lemon juice, shallot and peppercorns in a small
pan and bring to a bare simmer. Continue to simmer until the liquid
has reduced to about a tablespoon (this can happen quite fast, so don't
pick up the phone at this stage). Strain into a small bowl and leave to
cool completely.

In a glass or china bowl, whisk the egg yolks until really fluffy, using
an electric beater or rotary whisk. Add the vinegar reduction. Put the
bowl over a pan of simmering water – make sure the water doesn't touch
the bottom of the bowl. Then simply add the butter in small chunks,
whisking as you go. The two should emulsify into a thickish cream, just
like mayonnaise. Keep whisking as you add the butter until it is all used
up. Season to taste. You can keep the sauce in a warm place for half an
hour or so. If you put a circle of greaseproof paper on the top, any skin
that's formed will lift off with the paper when you're ready to serve.

Quick Tomato Sauce

This is one of those sauces that take less than 10 minutes to prepare and just half an hour to cook. It soon becomes a household staple. I make it in bulk and freeze it in relatively small portions – enough for two, say – so that I can whip it out for leftover suppers, especially pasta, pizzas, meat or fish balls, casseroles and bakes. It's a truly basic recipe, so feel free to tinker with the quantities of onion or garlic to suit your taste. You could add a big pinch of dried chilli flakes, a handful of basil or thyme or a couple of anchovy fillets, or pepper it with stoned black olives and rinsed capers. For a really gutsy pasta sauce, add a skinned, chopped chorizo or a small glass of red wine right at the start, once the onion has softened. You really can't go wrong with it.

When fresh tomatoes are cheap and in season, or when they are bursting from their growbag, use them in place of canned ones, for a paler, fresher-tasting sauce. You don't have to skin and deseed the tomatoes – just push the finished sauce through a sieve to get rid of the indigestible bits. I'd leave out the tomato purée and sugar too: when reduced down, really ripe tomatoes have their own sweetness and summery intensity.

The quantities below make enough for 2 generous servings of pasta.

a splash of olive oil
1 small to medium onion, chopped
1 large or 2 medium garlic cloves, finely chopped
400g can of chopped Italian tomatoes
2 teaspoons tomato purée
½ teaspoon caster sugar
salt and pepper

Heat the olive oil in a saucepan, add the onion and garlic and sweat for a couple of minutes so that they soften but do not colour. Add all the other ingredients and stir well, squashing down any tomato lumps to help break them up (if you want this sauce to cook quickly, strain the tinned tomatoes before using them – but I prefer to condense that liquid by cooking, which deepens the flavour). Bring the sauce to a very gentle simmer and cook slowly for 20–30 minutes, until it has reduced and thickened. You will need to stir it from time to time, and watch that it doesn't catch and burn at the bottom. Check the seasoning. Either use straight away or cool and store in the fridge (for 3–5 days) or freezer (for 3–4 months).

Marinades

Besides infusing meat with rich flavours, marinades can be really useful as a stay of execution for meat that should have been cooked the night before. You *could* put it in the freezer (but once defrosted it will need cooking immediately). Alternatively, when meat is just on the margin of its recommended use-by date, marinades are a quick and easy way of buying just enough time, safely.

Marinade ingredients fall into three groups: oils, which seal the meat from the air and carry the other flavours; acids, such as citrus fruit or vinegar, which help to tenderise the meat; and herbs and spices, which can be chopped or ground and added to cold oil or, as they do in India, warmed very gently in oil to release all their flavour. You can also add all sorts of flavourings such as honey, ketchup, soy sauce, horseradish or mustard. Speediest of all, you can use oil to thin down almost any ready-made pesto, curry paste or harissa for a very simple marinade.

Here are some ideas for marinades you can knock up fast depending on what you have to hand. To use any marinade, put the meat or fish in a shallow dish, coat it with the marinade, then cover with cling film and leave in the fridge for up to 8 hours, until you are ready to cook (fish would generally be marinated for a shorter time but if it's a question of making it last between breakfast and dinner, then a longer period is okay). Then remove it from its marinade, leaving some of the liquid and flavourings clinging to it, and grill, fry or roast it.

Use around 3 parts oil to 1 part vinegar or lemon. Exact quantities of herbs and spices don't matter but you won't need much more than around a tablespoon of chopped herbs or a good pinch of spice to give great flavour.

White fish marinades

- Thai curry paste thinned to a coating consistency with coconut milk
- Olive oil, dried oregano, chilli (flakes or fresh), lime or lemon juice
- Olive oil, ginger, garlic, a squeeze of lemon, chopped parsley or coriander

Oily fish marinades

- Olive oil, white wine vinegar, sliced white onion, bay leaf and a few whole peppercorns
- Olive oil, garlic, capers or chopped black olives, lemon juice, pepper
- White wine, soy sauce, grated fresh ginger, a splash of oil

Chicken marinades

- Olive oil, crushed garlic, lemon juice, chopped parsley, chopped thyme, sage or rosemary
- Olive oil, dried chilli flakes (or chopped fresh chilli), grated fresh ginger, chopped coriander and/or chopped mint
- Yogurt, a splash of olive oil, chopped basil and/or mint (you could add a dash of Tabasco to this, too, or a teaspoon of harissa paste from a tube)

Lamb marinades

- Harissa paste thinned to a coating consistency with olive oil
- Olive oil, crushed garlic, lemon juice, thyme or rosemary
- Olive oil, ground cumin, lemon juice, garlic

Beef marinades

- Equal amounts of runny honey and soy sauce, plus lime juice and crushed garlic (this also works for spare ribs or barbecued chicken)
- Olive oil, red wine, bay leaf
- Olive oil, black pepper and coriander seeds, both coarsely ground

Pork marinades

- Olive oil, crushed garlic, lemon juice, chopped thyme
- Olive oil, balsamic vinegar, bay leaf or chopped sage
- Olive oil, honey, grated fresh ginger, soy sauce

Preserves and Dips

Plain cold meat and fish are all inestimably nicer with a good robust chutney or pickle. Think of cold roast beef, spicy tomato chutney and a great fluffy baked potato filled with good butter; or cold lamb with a caper-y salsa verde. Leftover Christmas turkey and ham sandwiches positively sing with a great dollop of onion marmalade or chilli jam.

There are also times of the year when gluts of apples, tomatoes or soft fruit threaten to drown you with the spectre of imminent waste. Using them up (or taking advantage of their low price by buying a bagful) doesn't mean you have to turn yourself into a domestic factory, either. Chutneys benefit from keeping for at least six months and will last for several years: we don't have that brand of forbearance and usually have to ration them in the month or so before the time comes round to start all over again.

In the same spirit, a simple salsa verde or 'Bagnetto' (see page 46) will use up the last of a bunch of herbs (if you don't want to chop and freeze them) and there are easy dips that demolish languishing veggies. A mini-chopper makes all these not just easy but quick – and they will keep in the fridge for a couple of days, while dried tomatoes and peppers bottled in oil will last for a month or so.

These are leftovers' playmates – to gild a simple bit of crusty bread or lift a soup, salad, sandwich, bowl of rice or pasta or even a basic baked potato out of the ordinary. They're also one of my favourite ways of using up food – because they repay over and over again.

Storage tip

For foods designed to keep, like chutneys and jams, it's important to use a scrupulously well-washed jar, such as a Kilner, Parfait or jam jar, and to make sure that it doesn't already smell strongly of pickling spices. To sterilise the jar, use it straight from the dishwasher, or wash it out well with hot water and put it into the oven at 150°C/Gas Mark 2 for 15 minutes. Fill the jars before they cool and, with jams, place a wax disc (available from kitchen shops) on top before putting on the lid.

Basic Jam

You can make this jam with any glut of fruit. Under-ripe fruit has more pectin (which helps jam to set) but very ripe fruit can also be made into jam. I don't bother with special jam-making sugar, which contains added pectin – ordinary granulated does just fine. Make sure the fruit is dry first and prepare it by hulling, stoning or peeling it as usual. Raspberries, strawberries, gooseberries, plums, currants, blackberries, even rosehips and apples are all good – on their own or in combination. Jam should keep well for a year or so. Once you have opened the jar, if a thin mould forms you can scrape it off, along with about a centimetre of jam from below it, with no health dangers.

1

Use equal weights of white sugar to prepared fruit (see above). In a large pan, preferably stainless-steel, very gently heat the fruit and sugar together, stirring occasionally, until all the sugar has completely dissolved.

2

Turn up the heat and let the jam bubble quite rapidly, skimming off some of the foam that rises to the surface from time to time.

3

Depending on the fruit you use, boil it for 15–30 minutes, until a teaspoonful dolloped on to a fridge-chilled saucer sets within a minute or so, with a 'skin' on top. This is known as the 'setting point'.

4

Take out your warm, sterilised jars from
the oven or dishwasher (see page 39).

5

Pour the jam straight into the jars.

6

Cover the surface of each one with a wax disc
and a lid, and store in a cool, dark cupboard.

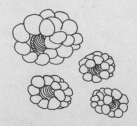

Onion Marmalade

Really handy for sandwiches, pies, soups and stews; just a teaspoon will add a deeply rich flavour to anything it touches. It's also great with a hard British cheese and it freezes well or keeps in the fridge for at least 2 weeks.

2 tablespoons olive oil
8–10 red or white onions, sliced as finely as possible
½ teaspoon dark muscovado sugar
1 tablespoon rich, syrupy balsamic vinegar (optional, but it adds
   sweetness and colour and helps the marmalade keep)

Heat the oil in a large, heavy-based frying pan, add the onions and fry over a high heat for 5 minutes, stirring constantly, so that they brown without burning. Turn the heat very low and add water just to cover. Bring to the boil and barely simmer for up to 1½ hours, until most of the water has evaporated and the onions are pulpy and soft. Add the sugar and stir until dissolved. Add the vinegar, if using, and simmer for 5–10 minutes. There should be almost no liquid left in the pan. Allow to cool, transfer to a warm sterilised jar (see page 39) and seal. Store in the fridge.

Stella's Apple Chutney

My gran made all sorts of chutneys but this is the one I love most. Rich with apples and spices, it clamours for cold meats or hard cheese.

2.3kg dessert apples, peeled, cored and diced
1.6kg soft dark brown sugar
850ml malt vinegar
900g onions, chopped
5 red chillies, deseeded and finely chopped
2½ teaspoons salt
2½ teaspoons ground ginger
1.2kg sultanas
½ teaspoon ground mixed spice

Put all the ingredients into a wide, heavy-based pan. Bring slowly to the boil and simmer gently for around 2½ hours, stirring occasionally. When you can draw a spoon through the mixture and it leaves a slight channel, the chutney is done. Fill warm sterilised jars (see page 39) with the hot chutney, seal and store for 6 months, if you have the patience.

Tomato Chutney

Because she knows I'm going to swipe half of it when my own has run out, my mother makes pots and pots of this chutney every year from her own tomatoes. It's perfect with baked potatoes, cold meat, sausages or barbecued chicken legs – or just with cheese on a thick slice of bread. Beware! Once you've tasted this chutney, you will wonder what you ever did without it.

1.8kg tomatoes, skinned and roughly chopped
900g dessert apples, peeled, cored and roughly chopped
450g onions, chopped
110g sultanas
2 teaspoons salt
¼ teaspoon ground black pepper
5cm piece of fresh ginger, grated
3 red chillies, deseeded and finely chopped
720ml malt vinegar
560g muscovado sugar
2 garlic cloves, finely chopped
1 tablespoon stem ginger in syrup, chopped, plus a tablespoon
  of its sugary juice (optional)

Put all the ingredients into a wide, heavy-based pan. Bring to the boil and simmer very gently for 2–2½ hours, stirring occasionally. When you can draw a spoon through the mixture and it leaves a slight channel, the chutney is done. Fill warm sterilised jars (see page 39) with the hot chutney, seal and keep for 6 months before use. Once you open the jars, store them in a cool place. Unopened chutney should keep for years.

Bottled Roasted Peppers

Roasted peppers are particularly delicious in pork stews or in a warm salad of Puy lentils, walnuts and goat's cheese with an oil and balsamic vinegar dressing. You'll find them incredibly versatile, and the advantage is that even slightly wilting peppers can be roasted and stored. I'm not a fan of green peppers, finding orange, yellow and red ones much sweeter and infinitely more digestible. They will keep in the fridge for a month or so if you store them in sterilised jars (see page 39).

Preheat the oven to 180°C/Gas Mark 4. Place the whole peppers on a baking tray and roast in the oven for about 30 minutes, until they are shrivelled and the skin cracks and blackens (even quicker, you can scorch them until black all over by putting them directly on to the gas burner on your hob). Put the roasted peppers straight into a plastic bag and tie the ends together – they will sweat as they cool, making peeling a doddle. When they are cool enough to handle, pull out the stalk and seeds, peel and rub off all the skin, then cut the flesh into strips. Place in a sterilised jar, cover with olive oil and seal.

Bottled Dried Tomatoes

I use the little cherry tomatoes that grow so easily in a growbag in the backyard and come all in a whoosh, leaving you casting around for new ideas on how to use them up. But any tomatoes will do. Like Bottled Roasted Peppers, they will keep in the fridge for a month or so if you store them in sterilised jars (see page 39).

Halve the tomatoes, arrange them on a baking tray and put into a very low oven – around 100°C, or the lowest possible gas mark – until they dry out, their flavour concentrating into little bursts of red sunshine. Don't rush it – the slower the oven, the more the juices will concentrate rather than run. It will take a couple of hours, but check them every now and then after the first hour and leave well alone until they begin to shrivel. Allow to cool, then place in a sterilised jar, cover with olive oil and seal.

Chilli Jam

A single jar of chilli jam will last for ages in or out of the fridge. It is intense enough for a scant teaspoon to add zing to stir-fries, sandwiches, seafood or – if you are a chilli fanatic – just about anything. The heat of all those chillies is mollified by the sugar syrup. You don't have to deseed the chillies but I think it works better if you do. Stored in a sterilised jar in the fridge, this will keep for several months.

170g red chillies
120g caster sugar
50ml white wine vinegar
40ml liquid pectin (available from chemist's or healthfood shops)

Slice the chillies open lengthwise and run a teaspoon down the centre of each one to remove the seeds (discard these). Chop the chillies as finely as you can, or pulse them in a mini blender (but stop before you turn them into a paste). Put them into a small, heavy-based pan with the sugar and vinegar, bring to the boil, stirring to dissolve the sugar, and simmer for 5 minutes. Remove from the heat, add the pectin and bring back to the boil. Simmer for 2 minutes, stirring constantly. Allow to cool a little and then store in a sterilised jar (see page 39).

Bagnetto

This is a Piedmontese salsa verde that goes beautifully with cold rare beef or lamb but is also extraordinarily good with fish such as cod, tuna or even mackerel, served cold. The point here is not to mince the ingredients so finely that they become a pesto-like paste but to keep a bit of hearty rusticity with slightly looser chopping, so that the ingredients maintain their own unique flavours and textures.

I would not make any salsa verde with the idea of keeping it, since its strong flavours and verdant colour will fade. Stored in an airtight plastic box, however, the sauce will keep in the fridge for a day or two.

a thick slice of white bread, crusts removed
2 tablespoons wine vinegar
leaves from a large handful of flat-leaf parsley, very finely chopped
10–15 salted capers, rinsed well and very finely chopped
1 teaspoon Dijon mustard
2 teaspoons finely chopped deseeded tomato,
  or 1 teaspoon tomato purée
2–4 anchovy fillets, according to taste, finely chopped
extra virgin olive oil

Soak the bread in the vinegar for a couple of minutes, then squeeze out the liquid (keep this) and chop the bread finely. Put it in a bowl, add all the other ingredients except the oil and vinegar and mix well. Slowly add enough olive oil to give the mixture a loose, spooning consistency rather than that of a pouring sauce. Finally drizzle the vinegar into the mixture.

You could also add...

- A finely sliced shallot and/or garlic clove and/or a little finely chopped gherkin, according to your taste.
- Other soft-leaved herbs, such as mint, dill, basil, tarragon and even coriander.

Ash's Spicy Carrot Pickle

This is one of those easy pickles that transform simple rice and leftover meat. The recipe was given to me by Ashutosh Khandekar, who, as far as I can make out, throws nothing away in his kitchen. The quantities below make just one small pot, but it is powerful stuff and you need only a little. It will last for ages in the fridge. Make more or less according to how many carrots you have lying around.

250g carrots, diced
1 teaspoon salt
juice of 1 lime or lemon
1 tablespoon sunflower oil
a pinch of asafoetida, if you can get it – and it makes a difference
1 heaped teaspoon black mustard seeds
½ teaspoon ground turmeric
½ teaspoon ground coriander
1 teaspoon red chilli powder

Mix the diced carrots with the salt and lime or lemon juice. Heat the oil in a pan, then add the asafoetida, if using, followed by the mustard seeds. Once the seeds begin to crackle, turn off the heat. Add the remaining spices and let them sizzle for a minute. Stir in the carrots, coating them well in the spicy oil.

Put the whole lot into a sterilised jar (see page 39) with a tight-fitting lid and leave in the fridge for a week or two before using.

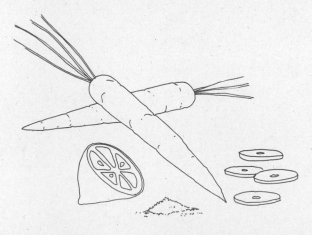

Guacamole

There's almost nothing else you can do with really ripe avocados –
though I wouldn't use them if the flesh is too bruised or brown.
This is a perfect dip for bread or raw vegetables and it's even good
with grilled salmon.

2 ripe avocados
1 tablespoon lemon juice
1 small garlic clove, chopped
1 small green chilli, deseeded and finely chopped (or about 5 drops
  of Tabasco sauce)
1 shallot or ¼ onion, very finely chopped
1 tablespoon olive oil
salt and pepper

Scoop out the flesh from the avocados and mash it with a fork, then
mix with all the other ingredients. Some people like their guacamole
a bit lumpy, others as smooth as face cream, so it's entirely up to you.
However you make it, do it at the last minute, because once the air hits
the avocado flesh, it discolours relatively fast.

Aubergine Dip

The single lonely aubergine in the bottom of the fridge needn't be
chucked when it can be turned into an amazing dip. Preheat the oven to
180°C/Gas Mark 4. Slice the aubergine into rounds about 1cm thick, put
these on an oiled baking tray and bake until tender. Then blitz them in
a food processor with a splash of olive oil, a little finely chopped garlic
and a squeeze of lemon juice to taste. Don't worry about peeling the
aubergine – the purple-black skin scorches nicely in the oven to give
a lovely deep, smoky flavour.

Bread

Here are some quick ways for using up the ends of bread and for making simple bread at home.

First, though, breadcrumbs: once you get into the habit of blitzing the ends of bread and freezing them, you'll discover that they come in endlessly handy – not least for the tops of bakes and gratins. The fact is that you can use any bread – the end of a fresh loaf, or stale slices – as long as it's not bone hard or mouldy. Leave on the crusts and simply blitz the whole lot into fine crumbs in a food processor or blender. Store in an airtight container in the fridge for up to a week or in the freezer for months.

Flavoured Breadcrumbs

Plain breadcrumbs are fine, but there are occasions when flavours can be added to give them an extra tang. This is the most basic recipe; you can jazz it up with capers, gherkins, extra garlic, a little chilli or any of your favourite chopped fresh herbs. Flavoured breadcrumbs don't keep so well, so make them as you need them, with either freshly made crumbs or your store from the freezer.

55g bread, made into crumbs
1 tablespoon chopped parsley
1 garlic clove, finely chopped
grated zest of 1 lemon
1 tablespoon freshly grated Parmesan cheese (optional, but really good
*   with chicken)*

Simply mix the whole lot together.

Emergency Bread

I often make up an emergency batch of crispy unleavened toast strips, not unlike pitta bread. It takes no longer than 10 minutes and, though a more gooey paste would be just as good for papier-mâché with the kids, these absolutely do the trick with soups or dips, especially for a Sunday supper.

Serves 4

250g plain flour
1 teaspoon salt
1 dessertspoon olive oil, plus extra for drizzling
150ml water

To garnish:
sea salt and black pepper

Preheat the oven to 200°C/Gas Mark 6. Sift the flour and salt into a bowl. Mix the oil and water together and pour about two-thirds into the flour, mixing well. Continue to add the liquid until you have a dough that easily holds together and does not stick to the side of the bowl; it should not be wet.

On a lightly floured surface, roughly knead the dough by pushing it downwards and away from you with one hand and flipping it back on to itself with the other. Every so often, give it a quarter turn. This should take only 2–3 minutes – just until the dough becomes smooth and elastic.

Roll out the dough to around 3mm thick. Prick it all over with a fork. Scatter a little sea salt and black pepper on top. Drizzle with a little olive oil and cut into strips, squares or circles. Place on a lightly oiled baking tray and bake for 5–7 minutes, until just turning lightly golden.

You could also...

o Add flavours to the dough before rolling: try a little dried thyme, paprika, finely sliced garlic, chopped black olives, a little chopped anchovy, lemon zest or even grated Parmesan.

Pitta Bread

If you are making a soup or dip and simply don't have any bread to serve with it, pittas will give the impression that you are a bit of a baking genius hiding your light under a bushel. Thrifty cooking is not necessarily about impressing, but what the hell …

Bear in mind that – with all that rising – pittas do take a bit of time to prepare. As with Emergency Bread, you can flavour them to your taste by adding a spoonful or two of your favourite flavouring, such as herbs or olives, to the dough.

Makes 8–10

370g plain flour
1 heaped teaspoon easy-blend yeast
2 teaspoons sea salt
50ml olive oil
200ml warm water

Sift the flour into a warm bowl and stir in the yeast and salt. Add the oil and about two-thirds of the water and mix well, then gradually add enough of the remaining water to make a claggy dough. Turn out on to a lightly floured surface and knead for 3 minutes or so, until the dough begins to feel soft and elastic. Cover and leave for 15 minutes, then knead again for 3 minutes. Transfer to a clean oiled bowl, cover with cling film and leave in a warm (but not hot) place to rise for an hour.

Knock back the dough by quickly punching out the air on a floured surface for a minute or so, then return it to the bowl, cover with cling film and leave to rise for a further hour or so, until doubled in size.

Divide the dough into 8–10 pieces and roll each into a ball. Cover with a damp tea towel and leave for half an hour – they will continue to rise.

Preheat the oven to 240°C/Gas Mark 9. Roll out each ball into a rough circle about 5mm thick. Place on non-stick baking trays and bake for around 4–5 minutes. The breads will puff up and begin to colour just lightly. Once they are ready, remove the pittas from the oven and leave to cool under a cloth or they will harden and crack.

Croûtons

There really is no point in buying croûtons when they cost practically nothing and take only a minute or two to make. Use up the stale ends of brown or white bread.

Cut the bread into 1cm dice (remove the crusts first, if you like). Heat some olive oil in a frying pan over a medium heat and when it is shimmering, toss in the bread, coating it with a little of the oil. Stirring occasionally, let the bread crisp and turn just golden on both sides. Remove from the pan and drain on kitchen paper. Add to soups or salads.

Other possibilities...

Flavoured croûtons You could flavour your croûtons by adding a little chopped garlic, herbs or chilli to the oil and letting it cook for barely a minute (being careful that it doesn't burn) before removing with a slotted spoon. Then use this flavoured oil for frying the bread.

Buttery croûtons Use butter instead of oil. Heat it until it is foaming but be careful that it does not burn – butter turns brown and bitter if overheated.

Soups

Soups are just about the simplest things to make, because they cook themselves while you get on with something else. They are the most natural way of using up leftovers or languishing vegetables – with, perhaps, a few extras from the store cupboard. They come in every colour and texture too, from an almost transparent broth to the deepest, chunkiest meal-in-a-bowl.

Soups almost always start with a chopped onion, a crushed clove of garlic and a little chopped carrot and/or celery, which are softened in oil before you add the main ingredient plus some stock or water. Once you've got the basic method taped, whatever you make will be limited only by the ingredients available and your own particular taste.

Home-made stock (see pages 27–30) really comes into its own now, especially if what you feel like eating is a simple, clear broth with just the addition of a handful of fresh herbs, a few shreds of leftover meat or fish or a couple of meatballs. In this case, follow the instructions for clarifying stock on page 29. Of course, you can use stock powder or cubes instead – just make them fairly dilute, and go easy when adding extra salt. Or, just use water – the flavour from the onion, carrot and celery with perhaps a bay leaf is often all you really need.

Texture is a matter of personal preference. If chunky soups are your thing, chop all the ingredients to your ideal size. For smooth soups, simply let the cooked soup cool and then blitz it. To serve, reheat the soup in a clean pan, but don't let it boil. If it looks too thick, thin it down with a little water or stock, or swirl in some cream or crème fraîche just before serving. But, if thickness is what you are after, add a diced potato or some starchy canned beans to the soup as it's cooking.

Soups taste even better the next day, though they often thicken up in the fridge and may need to be thinned with some stock, water or cream. And they freeze brilliantly, though be cautious with soups containing rice or pasta – the carbohydrate will just turn to mush. Remember that liquids expand when frozen, so don't overfill your bowl, bottle or bag.

Often at the very end of the culinary food chain, soups are also a fantastic way of using up leftover-leftovers. For example, if you make the Tomato, Chorizo and Chickpea Stew on page 74 and don't quite finish it, you'll find that overnight the flavours sink into each other and deepen. With a ladleful of stock or water, this will make an excellent soup – blitzed or chunky, as you like. Try doing this with almost any bake or stew.

Finally, most soups crave a partner: grated hard cheese, a spoonful of cream or plain yogurt, soft cheese such as goat's cheese, or a drizzling of good olive oil. No soup is at its best without warm crusty bread, plain toast or small cubes of bread gently fried to make croûtons (see page 52). Frozen breadcrumbs (see page 49), nuts or seeds can also be lightly toasted in a frying pan (keep them moving with a spoon in either case to prevent them burning) for scattering over the top.

It is worth bearing in mind two things when making soups: firstly, that you need to use a large pan: if you want a smooth soup, this will mean that you have room to blitz it all with a hand-held blender without it erupting like Vesuvius. Secondly, it stands to reason that if you use a pressure cooker your cooking time will be reduced, which is helpful for large amounts. (Follow the instructions that come with the cooker.)

Year-round Smooth Vegetable Soup

The multiple variations on this soup will take you right through the year, from autumn celeriac to summer beans and beetroot. Handy, then, not just for leftovers but for veggie-plot gluts or when fresh food is at its seasonal best and cheapest. Always make sure that the vegetables are cooked until they are completely tender or, when you blend the soup, you will have some pretty inedible lumps.

Makes 4–6 good-sized bowls or 8 small bowls

olive oil
1 onion, finely chopped
1 garlic clove, finely chopped
1 celery stick and/or carrot, chopped
1kg vegetables (cooked or uncooked), chopped
about 1.5 litres vegetable or chicken stock (see pages 27–30) or water
salt and pepper

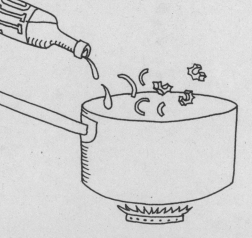

1

Heat a splash of olive oil in a large pan, add the onion, garlic and celery and/or carrot and cook gently, covered, for 5–7 minutes, until softened but not coloured.

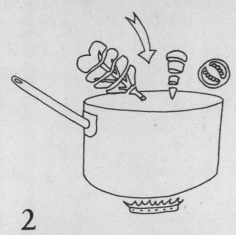

2

Add the vegetables, stir around and cook for 5 minutes.

3

Add enough stock or water just to cover, plus some salt and pepper, then simmer gently for 10 minutes, if using cooked vegetables, or about 20 minutes for raw vegetables.

4

Allow the soup to cool a little and then blitz to a creamy smoothness with a hand-held blender or in a liquidiser. Adjust the seasoning.

5

Reheat in a clean saucepan to serve.

ll list is impossible, but here are some of my favourite soups:

st vegetable Put anything leftover from a roast (including scraps of meat, if you like) into the pan after cooking the onion base. Pour over stock or water to cover, bring to a simmer and cook for 10 minutes, then blitz. Consider adding roasted red peppers or garlic, too.

Parsnip This is my husband David's take on a classic Jane Grigson recipe. Peel and dice the parsnips and add them to the onion base. Stir in ½ teaspoon of curry powder and cook very gently for 5 minutes. Add stock or water and simmer until the parsnips are tender. Blitz. Add 2 tablespoons of milk right at the end. Great with a dollop of black olive tapenade.

Root vegetable Carrots, potatoes, parsnips, swede, celeriac and turnips can be used on their own or in combination – with ½ teaspoon of curry powder or not, as you like, or a few sprigs of thyme and rosemary. Potato starch will make for a thick soup; add stock to thin things down.

Carrot Wonderful with a teaspoon of toasted and crushed caraway seeds or of grated fresh ginger added a minute or so before the liquid. It also works well if you use equal quantities of carrot and squash.

Pumpkin This is lovely if you add a good pinch of dried chilli flakes to the onion at the start. Use half coconut milk and half stock or water.

Celeriac and apple The mild tang of celeriac is gorgeous with the tart sweetness of apples. Add a medium potato to the base. For 1 medium celeriac use 2 eating apples, peeled and chopped. Serve with crisp bacon.

Pea or broad bean Simple and equally good hot in winter or cold in summer. Use either fresh or frozen vegetables. You could use a bunch of chopped spring onions instead of the usual onion base. Add peas or beans, then vegetable stock to cover, and simmer until entirely tender (or the skins will not purée properly). Blitz. If serving cold, squeeze in lemon juice to taste, scatter over some chopped mint, chervil or dill and stir in a dollop of crème fraîche. If serving hot, add a grating of good Parmesan and some lightly fried garlic croûtons (see page 52) or crisp bacon pieces.

Broccoli Works well lifted with a squeeze of lemon before serving and a plateful of chunky brown toast, each slice rubbed on one side with a peeled raw garlic clove. You could also use up the ends of blue cheese here by stirring them in gently just before serving.

Cauliflower Grate a 2–3cm piece of fresh ginger into the onion base.

Potato and leek Use equal amounts of diced potato and leek (floury potatoes are best) and a good vegetable or mild chicken stock, or a half-and-half mix of stock and milk. Purée and serve hot or cold.

Potato and watercress or spinach With a good grating of nutmeg, this is sublime. Serve with chopped fresh coriander and a dollop of soft goat's cheese. It's also good with leftover sausage, chorizo or bacon.

Beetroot For 4 peeled and grated beetroot, use a crushed clove of garlic and a litre of stock to cover. Simmer until the purple strips are entirely tender (which can take longer than you expect). Serve with a squeeze of lemon juice, a dollop of crème fraîche and some chopped mint. Being unorthodox, I prefer to purée beetroot soup until it is so thick that it can practically be eaten with a fork. In this case, some toasted bread rubbed with a raw clove of garlic is essential.

Cabbage and bacon Use smoked bacon, or the end of a joint of ham, cooked with the onion at the start. Odd though it sounds, ¼ teaspoon of ground cumin for 1 small cabbage will lift the soup out of the ordinary. Sprinkle over crisp diced bacon to serve.

Tomato Drop the tomatoes into a big bowl of just-boiled water for a minute and the skins will peel off easily. Chop roughly, discarding the seeds. Simmer in stock (or half and half with milk for a creamier result) and serve with a dollop of soured cream and some chopped basil or chives.

Two Chunky Vegetable
Soups for Summer or Winter

These Italian soups are the best when it comes to using up spring and summer vegetables or hearty winter leaves in a delicious and satisfying broth. Minestrone and ribollita are similar in technique but vary in ingredients – minestrone being the summery cousin and ribollita the one I crave on the return from a long, cold walk. They are both endlessly variable according to what you have to hand.

Ribollita

Ribollita means re-boiled, so this warming, hearty soup was *invented* to use up leftover food, especially pulses. Traditionally, it is made with the dark Italian cabbage called cavolo nero but it is just as good with Swiss chard, kale or purple sprouting broccoli. Don't worry too much if you don't have all the ingredients listed below – the soup will not suffer.

Serves 4

*olive oil for frying (and some extra virgin olive oil for drizzling
    on the top)*
1 large red onion, chopped
2 garlic cloves, chopped
1 head of celery, chopped (include the leaves)
4 carrots, chopped
leaves from a bunch of parsley, chopped
400g can of plum tomatoes, drained
*a big bunch of cavolo nero, kale or purple sprouting broccoli,
    finely shredded*
400g can of white beans, such as butterbeans, cannellini or borlotti
½–1 loaf of stale baguette, ciabatta or similar bread, torn into chunks
salt and pepper

Heat a generous splash of olive oil in a large saucepan or frying pan, add the onion and garlic and cook gently until softened. Then add the celery, carrots and parsley and toss the whole lot well to coat it in the oil. Cook gently for 5–7 minutes, until the carrots are beginning to soften. Add the tomatoes (snip them with scissors if they are not already chopped) and cook for 10 minutes. Add the cavolo nero, kale or broccoli and the can of beans, with enough of the liquid from the can just to cover the greens. You may need to add a little hot water from the kettle, but don't swamp it. Simmer gently for 10–15 minutes, until the greens are just tender. Add the bread, season to taste and then serve with a good drizzle of extra virgin olive oil. The soup should be chunky with a pool of liquid – just enough to hold it all together.

More possibilities...

Bearing in mind that the spirit of this soup lies in the juxtaposition of starch (the beans) and the strong greens, and in the dance between chunky texture and lip-smacking broth, you could also experiment with:

Other green vegetables Substitute peas, spinach or finely shredded cabbage for the cavolo nero.

Bottled artichoke hearts and frozen broad beans A delicious combination to replace the cavolo nero and beans, giving a slight hint of summer. Just before serving, stir in a good handful of finely chopped herbs, such as mint, parsley or coriander.

Fennel and broad beans These work well together too. For a meatier kick, just add some bits of lightly browned bacon or torn-up prosciutto before serving.

Chickpeas and diced chorizo Skin the chorizo and dice or crumble it. Cook it with the onion at the start until its oily juices begin to run. Use canned chickpeas in place of the beans. This makes a marvellously robust soup and the tang of the greens chimes deliciously with the spicy chorizo.

Minestrone

Minestrone is less gutsy than ribollita, relying on pasta rather than bread and fresh peas or beans rather than dried pulses. It's a lighter way of using up courgettes, peas, small broad beans or early French beans and, though the ingredients list below may look daunting, it's really up to you what you put in. In general, the smaller you dice the vegetables, the better.

If you're using fresh tomatoes, remove the skins first by letting them sit in just-boiled water for one minute and then pricking them with the point of a knife. The skin should burst open, allowing you to peel it off easily. If it doesn't, leave the tomatoes for a little longer. Roughly chop them before adding them to the soup, discarding the seeds if you like.

It is traditional to use up small amounts of leftover cooked pasta in this soup – either small macaroni or fine spaghettini or linguine, cut into lengths of about 2.5 cm. Equally, you could use leftover rice or a small amount of cooked beans or pulses, such as chickpeas or cannellini beans. Just add any of these to the broth a minute before serving.

There's nothing to stop you adding some fine strips of leftover poultry to the soup right at the end.

Serves 4

1 onion, finely chopped
1 large garlic clove, crushed
olive oil
2 celery sticks, chopped into slim half-moons
1 leek, finely sliced, and/or 1 fennel bulb, diced, its leaves finely chopped
2 new potatoes, peeled and cut into small dice
1 litre vegetable or chicken stock (see pages 27–30)
2 courgettes, cut into small dice
about 400g early-summer peas or French beans (or both)
2 large or 3 small tomatoes, skinned and chopped (optional)
a handful of linguine, broken into pieces about 2.5cm long (optional)
salt and pepper

To serve:
about 2 teaspoons Pesto (see page 139)
extra virgin olive oil
freshly grated Parmesan cheese

Sweat the onion and garlic in a little olive oil until softened, then add the celery, leek and/or fennel. When these have softened, add the potatoes and stock. Bring to the boil and simmer for 10–15 minutes, until the potatoes are just tender, then add the remaining vegetables and simmer gently for 10 minutes. If you want to add the linguine, do so at the same time as the peas and beans, checking that it is properly cooked before serving. Season to taste.

Serve with ½ teaspoon of pesto swirled into each bowl, plus a drizzle of really good olive oil, a generous grating of Parmesan cheese and some crusty bread.

Meat Soups

These are hearty soups, so blitz them as much or as little as you like or – as with the Pea and Bacon Soup on page 64 – not at all. Keep back a few strips of meat to add to a smooth soup at the last minute, or use a potato masher to achieve a semi-puréed texture. The very last scraps of the meat will provide all you really need but whatever texture you are after, always carefully remove every bit of fat and gristle.

These soups will benefit if you use stock made from the bones or carcass of the meat (see pages 28–9). Bear in mind that leftover meat or fish will not give up much more flavour and overcooking it will make it dry and tough, so this is all much quicker than cooking it from scratch.

For meat soups, I tend to add an equal measure of companionable vegetables – or canned pulses and beans really come into their own as alternative thickeners to potatoes. Bottled Roasted Peppers or Dried Tomatoes (see page 44) will add kick. Either cook them with the meat and stock or add them right at the end as a garnish. Use the What Goes With What list on pages 26–7 for inspiration if you are unsure.

Pea and Bacon Soup

I boil a bacon joint fairly regularly and it is worth buying a slightly larger piece of meat just in order to make this soup. It's an ancient pairing of flavours and, though I prefer green peas, you could more authentically use the same quantity of cooked split peas or even lentils.

Serves 4

a little olive oil
1 onion, chopped
1 carrot, diced
1 celery stick, sliced
1 bay leaf
300–400g fresh or frozen petits pois
300–400g (about 4 teacups) leftover ham, cut into pieces
about 1.5 litres meat or vegetable stock (see pages 27–30)
100–150ml cream
salt and pepper
a handful of chopped fried bacon, to serve

Heat a splash of olive oil in a large pan, add the onion, carrot and celery and cook gently, covered, for 5–7 minutes, until softened but not coloured. Add the bay leaf, peas and ham and cover with the stock. Bring to the boil and simmer gently for 5–7 minutes, until the peas are really tender. Check the seasoning (ham is salty, so be careful before adding more) and add cream to taste. Scatter some chopped fried bacon on top.

Delicious combinations for meat soups...

For these variations, cook raw vegetables right at the beginning with the onion and add the meat only when they are completely cooked through. If you are using up leftover cooked vegetables, add them to the liquid once it has reached simmering point, along with the leftover meat. Simmer for 5–7 minutes, until all the ingredients are thoroughly heated.

Chicken, leek and mushroom Replace the onion and bay leaf with some finely sliced leeks and a little chopped garlic, rosemary or thyme. Add some sliced mushrooms. Once these are cooked, add half a cup of milk with the water or stock and, when it is simmering, add strips of leftover chicken and simmer until thoroughly heated through. A squeeze of lemon and some fine strips of lemon zest added at the end will brighten it up, or scatter over some chopped tarragon, parsley or basil.

Chicken or pork (roast, boiled or even sausages) These go well with lentils or chickpeas (canned ones are fine). Add a good handful of chopped parsley at the end. If you have a few tomatoes lying around, skin, deseed and chop them and add them to the soup with the meat.

Ham or pork (including sausages) Both taste good with strong green vegetables. Add a couple of crushed garlic cloves to the onion base and use any member of the cabbage family, shredded finely. When cooked, add the meat. Shredded fennel is a summer alternative.

Lamb and pulses Lamb is delicious with butterbeans, cannellini beans, chickpeas or even frozen broad beans. A teaspoon of harissa from a tube can be stirred into the onion base before adding the meat and beans. Serve with a little chopped fresh coriander or parsley.

Beef with root vegetables Beef is a natural partner for sweet root vegetables such as potatoes, parsnips, celeriac and carrots. Tomatoes (skinned and chopped) will add a tangy sweetness.

Beef with summer vegetables Try a base of softened leeks and celery, adding diced raw courgettes and even aubergine, and then the stock. Add strips of leftover beef to warm through. A teaspoon of paprika, ground cumin or ground coriander would be nice added at the start.

Christmas leftover soup Because there is so much to play with – turkey or duck, the end of a ham, roast parsnips and potatoes, a bit of bacon or sausage, green vegetables and stuffings – you can do away with the onion/carrot/celery base, and use cold water instead of stock. Even the last of the bread sauce or cranberry sauce can go into the pot. Blitz and serve with finely sliced spring onions or chopped coriander leaves.

Clear Broths

These are the kind of soups that come together in literally minutes – almost instant soups whose transparency and minimalism leave you feeling healthily satisfied, whether you've made a socking great bowlful with noodles or an abstemious little dish lightly scented with fresh herbs. Home-made stock is best, clarified following the instructions on page 29.

Lamb Balls in Broth

My husband often makes Kofta (see page 146) – slightly spicy little Lebanese lamb balls, which include parsley, a little chopped red pepper and the gentle nuzzle of a pinch of ground cinnamon. They are ideal for this soup, but any leftover meatballs will do (see pages 144–5). It's a Sunday-night delight – endlessly adaptable and taking just 10 minutes to prepare.

For a more aromatic, less Middle Eastern approach, leave out the cinnamon and add a bruised cardamom pod to the broth, remembering to remove it before serving.

Serves 2

about 850ml good clarified stock, ideally lamb or beef (see pages 28–9)
a good pinch of ground cinnamon
30–50g uncooked basmati rice, or 1 teacup leftover cooked rice
6–10 small meatballs (see pages 144–5)
a handful of fresh coriander or parsley, finely chopped
salt and pepper

Bring the stock to simmering point and add the cinnamon. Stir well and, if using raw rice, add it now. Simmer until the rice is a couple of minutes off being cooked. Add the meatballs and heat through thoroughly. If you're using cooked rice, add it now. Season with salt and pepper, add the herbs and serve immediately, accompanied by flatbreads and a green salad.

More possibilities...

Chicken ball broth Use chicken or vegetable stock and add a couple of sliced bottled artichoke hearts per person. Before serving, add a squeeze of lemon, some really finely chopped chives or spring onions and a scattering of tender young parsley leaves.

Pork ball broth Use a light meat or vegetable stock and omit the cinnamon. Fennel sliced so thinly that it is almost transparent would be a great addition, or very finely shredded cabbage.

Beef ball broth Leave out the cinnamon and use beef stock, if you have it. Add skinned, deseeded and chopped tomatoes to the broth as it simmers. (Instead of beef balls you could use herb dumplings – see page 135.)

Leftover risotto broth Elizabeth David gave a recipe for using cooked risotto in a soup, which sounds strange but is heavenly. Make small balls from the leftover risotto, adding chopped herbs if you like. Dip the risotto balls in egg and breadcrumbs, fry them in a little oil and then slip them into a simple chicken or vegetable broth (see Arancini, pages 140–1).

Leftover fish broth Omit the meatballs and cinnamon, use fish stock and add a few defrosted Atlantic prawns, if you have them, quickly poached in the stock. Right at the end, drop in some pieces of leftover fish, just to warm though. Add a skinned, deseeded and chopped tomato, shredded baby spinach or fine rice noodles for variety.

Leftover meat broth Tear leftover meat into strips and add them to a pan of simmering broth, giving them just enough time to heat through before serving.

Noodle broth Add some egg or rice noodles, plus a handful of spinach, sliced mushrooms or Chinese leaves, to a pan of simmering broth and cook until they are just tender. Serve with some finely chopped spring onions.

Smoked Fish Soup

The classic smoked fish soup is Scottish cullen skink, made with smoked haddock. Frankly, though, you can use just about any kind of smoked fish you have to hand, even oily fish such as kippers and mackerel. Indeed, the leftovers of a fish pie, thinned with a little milk and stock, warmed and blitzed in a blender, would make a fine alternative. If you are using leftover cooked fish and you don't have any of your own fish stock (see page 30), it is worth buying some from your local fishmonger or supermarket. Like all soups, this one freezes well.

Serves 4

a little oil or butter
1 onion, chopped
450g smoked fish fillet (cooked or raw)
about 570ml water (if using raw fish) or fish stock (if using cooked fish)
225g leftover mashed potato
570ml milk
salt and pepper
cream or crème fraîche, to serve
a handful of parsley or chives, chopped, to serve

Heat a little oil or butter in a pan, add the onion and cook until softened. If you are using raw fish, add it to the pan, cover with water and simmer for 2–3 minutes. Remove the fish, allow it to cool, then remove the skin and check for bones. Break the flesh into large pieces and keep separate. The liquid in the pan forms the stock for the soup.

If you are using cooked fish, skin it, break the flesh into rough chunks and put on one side. Pour the fish stock over your onion base and bring to a slow simmer.

Stir the mashed potato into the simmering liquor and whisk until smooth. Add the milk and then add the fish. Simmer very gently for 3 minutes maximum, just to heat the fish through. Season to taste and serve each portion topped with a dollop of cream or crème fraîche and some chopped parsley or chives, accompanied by warm crusty bread.

Stews and Curries

The best stews (or casseroles, or whatever you want to call them) are made from scratch with raw meat or vegetables, wonderfully seasoned and cooked very, very slowly. The great thing about them is that they transform cheap cuts of meat into meltingly tender cold-weather comfort food – and they are practically impossible to mess up. Whatever is left over can be frozen for a ready meal later on or thinned with some good-quality stock and blitzed into a hearty soup.

If you have a fair bit of meat left over, though, there's absolutely nothing wrong with making a stew with it – using up wilting vegetables at the same time. Unlike classic stews made from scratch, these are relatively fast, taking minutes rather than hours. As with soups (see pages 53–68), you start with a good base of softened onion and garlic, bulk up the meat with companionable vegetables, add the flavour and freshness of herbs and swathe the whole lot in a gravy made from stock, a can of tomatoes or other liquid.

Curries, whether you use a fresh array of spices or a ready-made curry powder or paste, are quick and almost effortless – certainly nothing exotically untoward – and if you keep them on the mild side most children will find them thrillingly different and gobble them up.

It's worth repeating that cooked meat has already given up most of its juices and will only toughen if cooked again for too long. So with these dishes, the normal order of things is reversed: generally, the meat is added at the last minute, once the gravy or sauce has cooked and thickened, and it's left only for as long as it takes to heat through completely. Remember that stews, like soups, can be among your very best friends in terms of combining flavours – almost anything goes. If you don't find what you are looking for in the lists of variations here, you can easily adapt the basic process by taking inspiration from the recipes for soups on pages 53–68, or by using the What Goes with What list on pages 26–7.

An Infinitely Adaptable Stew

I've chosen chicken and paprikary tomato here because it takes me straight back to my childhood, when this stew was so much a part of my mother's repertoire that she often cooked a larger chicken than we could possibly eat just in order to have enough left over to make it. Beef, pork or lamb could be used instead. For any stew, trim the meat well of fat and gristle, tearing it into pieces at least 'double-bite-sized' so that they don't fall apart while cooking.

You can add virtually anything, and you don't need to be precise with quantities – it all depends on how much meat you have to work with. Use a home-made tomato sauce (see page 36) or leave out the tomatoes entirely and replace them with good meat or vegetable stock (see pages 27–30), or even some leftover soup, blitzed until smooth and thinned with water or stock. The idea is to build something that uses your favourite (available) tastes in combination – often the kind of partnerships listed on pages 26–7.

Serves 4

a little oil
1 onion, finely chopped
2 large garlic cloves, crushed
about 450g cooked chicken, in chunks and/or joints
a bay leaf or bouquet garni
400g can of chopped tomatoes
1 dessertspoon tomato purée
1 rounded teaspoon paprika
soured cream or yogurt
salt and pepper

1

In a largish, heavy-based casserole, heat a little oil, then add the onion and garlic and cook gently, covered, for a few minutes, until softened but not coloured.

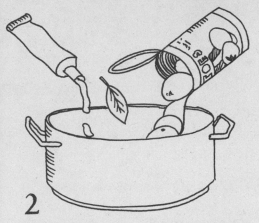

2

Add the bay leaf or bouquet garni, chopped tomatoes, tomato purée, paprika and salt and pepper.

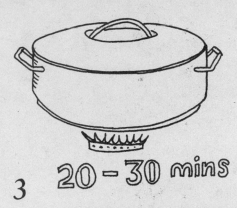

3

Bring to the boil, cover and leave to bubble very slowly either on the hob or in a moderate oven (around 180°C/Gas Mark 4).

4

After 20–30 minutes, when the tomatoes have reduced to a good thickness, remove from the heat, adjust the seasoning and take out the bay leaf or bouquet garni.

5

Add the chicken (but don't break chunks of chicken flesh too small or you will get a mush of fibres rather than a chunky stew). Simmer for 3–5 minutes, until thoroughly heated through.

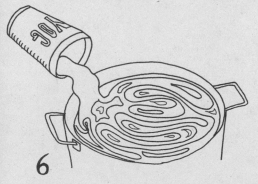

6

Remove from the heat and stir in a great glug of soured cream or yogurt, swirling it round so that the colours are marbled like hand-made Venetian writing paper.

7

Serve with steamed rice (half wild and half basmati is really nice here) and a crisp green salad or French beans.

Lots of alternative stews...

Chicken 'puttanesca' Add some chopped anchovies to the onion, then 1–2 teaspoons of capers and/or a teacup of good black olives with the chicken. This is great with rice or potatoes and equally glorious on pasta.

Chickpeas, cannellini beans or butterbeans The gutsy flavour of reduced tomatoes is always good balanced by the floury starchiness of these pulses. Add a drained 400g can of beans with the tomatoes.

Tomato, chorizo and chickpeas Chickpeas are astonishingly good with chorizo or sausages and make a great stew with or without the addition of the chicken. Chop the chorizo into generous-sized pieces and cook it slowly with the onion until it starts to break apart and release its red oil – a good 10 minutes. Add the chickpeas with the tomatoes. Or use potatoes instead, peeled and diced to the same size as the chorizo chunks, and cook for 30–40 minutes, until the potatoes are tender. Omit the soured cream or yogurt and serve with a good handful of grated Parmesan.

A North African twist Use either chicken or pork and replace the canned tomatoes with enough chicken stock just to cover the meat. Add a handful of raisins, a finely sliced fennel bulb, the zest of an orange, a teaspoon of chilli flakes and a stick of cinnamon. Serve with rice and chopped mint.

Root vegetables Leave out the meat entirely and substitute a similar quantity of root vegetables, such as potato, sweet potato, parsnip, carrot, pumpkin, turnip – all peeled and cut into chunks of about the same size so that they cook evenly. Add with the onion and garlic.

Leftover lamb or beef Replace the chicken with diced leftover lamb or beef and use red onion instead of white at the start. Add ½ teaspoon of paprika to the onion once soft, cooking it for 30 seconds or so before adding the tomatoes. Leave these to reduce and thicken, then add white beans, chickpeas or leftover cooked potatoes. Add the meat 6 or 7 minutes before serving, along with a couple of good handfuls of baby spinach and/or a handful of coriander leaves.

Moroccan-style Stew

This fake 'tagine' works well with any meat, though lamb is perhaps the most delicious with this clinging, sweet and winey sauce. Or you could forget the meat and use root vegetables instead, adding them with the onion marmalade at the start.

Serves 3–4

a little oil
2 rounded tablespoons Onion Marmalade (see page 42)
1 teaspoon each of ground cumin and ground ginger
a good pinch of ground cinnamon
6 garlic cloves, peeled but left whole
2 tablespoons each of stoned black olives and capers, drained and rinsed
180ml red wine
180ml water or mild stock
250g dried fruits – a mixture of apricots and prunes is lovely
4 teacups (400–500g) cooked lamb, trimmed and cut into pieces
salt and pepper

In a heavy-based pan, gently heat a little oil and the onion marmalade. Stir in the cumin, ginger and cinnamon and cook for 1 minute. Add all the other ingredients except the meat, stir well and cover. Cook slowly on the hob or in a low oven (150°C/Gas Mark 2) for 40 minutes or so, until the sauce has reduced by a good third. Add the meat and heat through for 10 minutes. Season to taste. Serve with couscous and a green salad.

Consider also...

Pork or chicken Substitute pork or chicken for the lamb, use green instead of black olives and white instead of red wine, and add a lemon, cut into 8 segments, or some preserved lemon. Serve with chopped parsley.

Beef Substitute beef for the lamb and add several raw potatoes, peeled and cut into smallish pieces, right at the start with the onion marmalade. Leave out the capers. Chunks of fennel could also be added with the potatoes.

Two Creamy Middle Eastern Dishes

These very gentle Middle Eastern dishes give you something entirely different for your leftovers repertoire, using yogurt or sesame paste (tahini) to make a caressingly creamy sauce into which you slip the meat or fish. I learned how to make them from the cookery writer Anissa Helou, whose thoughtful dishes are always incredibly healthy, as well as delicious. Serve with warm flatbreads, chopped basil or coriander and a green salad.

Fish with Tahini

This Lebanese dish is most often prepared with whole fish but you can also use leftover fish.

> Serves 2
>
> *100ml tahini (sesame paste)*
> *115ml water*
> *juice of 1 large lemon*
> *a little vegetable oil*
> *2 onions, thinly sliced*
> *2 teacups (about 200g) leftover fish, flaked*
> *salt*

Put the tahini in a mixing bowl and gradually stir in the water and lemon juice until you have a pale liquid the consistency of a thin, creamy soup. Add a little more water if it looks too thick.

Pour a little vegetable oil into a frying pan over a medium heat, add the onions and fry until golden. Add the tahini and salt to taste, then allow to bubble until you see a little oil rising. Turn off the heat and slip the fish gently into the sauce. Serve tepid or at room temperature.

Lamb in Cooked Yogurt Sauce

This recipe can be used as a basis for cooking other meat in yogurt, varying the taste by replacing the coriander with mint or basil. Indeed, you could make it entirely vegetarian by using a can of chickpeas or some cooked cauliflower florets or diced courgettes in place of the lamb.

What rescues this deliciously mild and velvety dish from blandness is the pungency of the garlic and the aromatic hit of the herbs. For a slightly thicker sauce, you could omit the stock.

Serves 2

1 heaped teaspoon soft butter
a small bunch of fresh coriander, finely chopped
1 large garlic clove, finely chopped
500g plain yogurt (even better if you can find the thick, curdy yogurt
   freshly made daily in some Middle Eastern grocery stores)
1 egg, lightly whisked
2 teacups (about 200g) leftover lamb, fat and gristle removed,
   torn into good-sized pieces
the white heads of 8 spring onions
210ml stock (optional – if you are after a thicker sauce, leave it out)
salt and pepper

Melt the butter in a small frying pan over a medium heat, add the coriander and garlic and sauté for a minute until the garlic is softened but not browned. Remove from the heat and set aside.

Put the yogurt in a heavy-based pan, add the whisked egg and mix well. Bring gently to the boil, stirring regularly to prevent curdling, then turn down the heat and simmer for 3 minutes, still stirring.

Now add the meat to the yogurt sauce, along with the spring onions and the garlic and coriander mixture. Add the stock, if using. Simmer gently for 3 minutes. Serve immediately, with vermicelli or rice.

Lamb or Beef Ragù

Neither casserole nor curry, this ragù transforms the idea of a 'Bolognese' into a meltingly tasty sauce for pasta or to eat on its own with rice. Kids love it, it freezes well and you can turn the last bowlful into a great lunchtime soup by thinning it with a little stock or water and blitzing in a blender.

Always prepare the meat well first by trimming off all fat and gristle and chopping or mincing it very finely. If you are doing this in a food processor, use the pulse button: you really don't want to turn the meat into a paste.

I prefer not to drain the tomatoes for this sauce as, when cooked at a slow bubble, all the liquid reduces, leaving behind its flavour. If you are in a hurry, though, do strain the tomatoes.

Serves 2

a little butter or olive oil
1 onion, finely chopped
1 good-sized garlic clove, crushed
1 bay leaf
a sprig of thyme, if you have it
400g can of chopped tomatoes
1 tablespoon tomato purée
2 teacups (about 200g) leftover roast lamb or beef,
  finely chopped or minced
salt and pepper

Heat a little butter or olive oil in a saucepan, add the onion and garlic and cook gently until softened. Add all the other ingredients except the meat, stir well and bring to simmering point. Turn down the heat and leave the ragù to bubble, just barely, for 25–35 minutes, until it has thickened and deepened in colour. Add the meat and cook for 2–3 minutes, until heated through.

Other possibilities...

Enrich or spice up the sauce Add a glass of red wine or a pinch of dried chilli flakes once the onion is cooked and leave the wine to bubble for 2–3 minutes before adding the tomatoes. Use up a last rasher of bacon – dicing it and adding it with the onion at the start. Or toss in some finely chopped parsley or basil right at the end.

Carrots, parsnips or courgettes Add these in small dice to the tomatoes and cook until softened before adding the meat. If your children rebel against chunks of vegetables, grate them.

An echo of the East Grate a 2.5cm piece of fresh ginger and add to the onion at the start with a deseeded and chopped small green chilli and a teaspoon each of ground coriander and cumin. Scatter chopped coriander over the finished ragù and serve with rice or couscous.

Ratatouille

Ratatouille uses up all the tomatoes, courgettes and aubergines that mock you from the vegetable rack or the fridge. It freezes well, and is one of those dishes that taste even better the next day – and it can ultimately make its way into either a bake with a breadcrumb topping (see page 49) or a soup.

Serves 4

1 large aubergine, sliced into rounds about 1cm thick
olive oil
1 large red onion, chopped
4 garlic cloves, chopped
2–4 courgettes, sliced about 5mm thick
1 large pepper, deseeded and sliced
    (or use Bottled Roasted Peppers, see page 44)
450g tomatoes, skinned and roughly chopped
    (or a 400g can of tomatoes, drained and chopped)
1 heaped teaspoon tomato purée
1 tablespoon chopped basil (or thyme)
1 tablespoon chopped flat-leaf parsley
1 teaspoon chopped oregano (if you have it)
salt and pepper

Brush the aubergine slices with olive oil and then grill (or bake at 180°C/Gas Mark 4) for about 10 minutes, until golden and tender, flipping them over half way through. Allow to cool and then chop into chunks.

Fry the onion gently in a little oil in a large saucepan until soft. Add the garlic and cook for a further 30 seconds or so. Add more oil if you need to and then throw in the courgettes. Cook, turning regularly, until they become translucent and are just beginning to brown. Add the aubergine, pepper, tomatoes and tomato purée and season well. Simmer very gently for 30–45 minutes, until the vegetables are soft but not disintegrating and the sauce is thickening, without becoming a pulp.

Adjust the seasoning and stir in the chopped herbs. Serve on its own, or with rice, pasta, couscous or baked potatoes, or as a side dish with chicken, lamb, pork or fish. Ratatouille also goes perfectly with a poached egg.

A cold-weather alternative Carrots, potatoes, broccoli, cauliflower and any member of the squash family can be used for a wintry version of ratatouille. In this case, I prefer to leave the vegetables quite chunky. Start in the same way with onion and garlic, adding the harder vegetables next and turning them in the oil until partially softened. Add the tomatoes and tomato purée, season well and simmer until the vegetables are almost cooked. About 10 minutes before you want to serve, add softer vegetables such as broccoli, cauliflower, and some mangetout or beans.

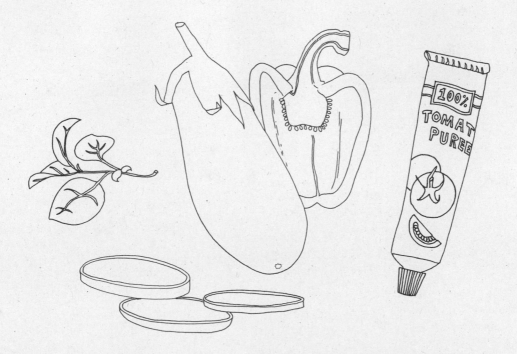

Two Indian Curries,
Depending on Your Fortitude

All curries are endlessly variable. You can use a good teaspoon of curry paste or your own spices, as below; experiment to find out what you prefer and how strong you like them. Coconut milk, yogurt or a can of tomatoes can form the basis of the sauce or, if you want a really mild curry, ordinary milk works beautifully.

The absolute rule with these curries is always, always to cook the spices for a good minute or two before adding the liquid. This will take off their raw edge and intensify the flavour. If you want to use fresh meat, you will need to add it to the pan before the liquid, turning it well over a fairly high heat until it has coloured on all sides. With leftover meat, though, the opposite is the case – you need to build up the flavours and thicken the sauce before tossing in your meat to warm through right at the end.

Simple Mild Curry
– Best for Poultry, Fish or Vegetables

This is a gentle, well-behaved curry. You can play around with the spices as you like: substitute a rounded teaspoon of curry paste or powder for the individual spices used below or replace them with gentler spices such as cumin or coriander seeds – well toasted and then bashed in a mortar – or bruised cardamom pods, fenugreek and fennel seeds along with the ginger and garlic. With mild curries like these, a final squeeze of lemon adds real brightness and a generous handful of toasted flaked almonds will give a sweet crunch.

When it comes to vegetable curries, take inspiration from your favourite Indian restaurant; sweet potatoes and pumpkin are particularly fine together; mushrooms pair deliciously with green beans.

Serves 2

1 onion, chopped
2 garlic cloves, crushed
2 teaspoons grated fresh ginger
a little butter or oil
1 teaspoon ground turmeric
1½ teaspoons garam masala
a small pinch of chilli powder (or more, to taste)
2 ripe tomatoes, skinned and chopped
½ teacup coconut milk or yogurt
about 2 teacups (200g) diced leftover poultry, fish or vegetables
    of your choice (or fresh meat, fish or vegetables)
a handful of chopped fresh coriander

Sauté the onion, garlic and ginger in a little butter or oil until just
beginning to colour. Add the turmeric, garam masala and chilli
(or replace these with curry paste or powder) and cook gently for
1–2 minutes to open up the flavour of the spices.

If you are using fresh meat, fish or vegetables, add them now and
turn them in the spiced onion mixture until well coated. Then stir in
the tomatoes, followed by the coconut milk or yogurt (which will
separate slightly into delicious curds) and bring gently to the boil.
Cook at a lazy bubble for about 8 minutes if using chicken or fish,
more like 20 for vegetables.

If you are using leftover meat, fish or vegetables, add the tomatoes
to the spiced onion mixture, followed by the yogurt, and let the curried
sauce bubble away for about 15 minutes, until thickened. Then slip the
meat, fish or vegetables into the pan and simmer gently for 5 minutes or
so, until they are thoroughly heated through.

Sprinkle the chopped coriander over the curry and serve with rice,
salad or flatbreads, plus mango chutney, plain yogurt or yogurt mixed
with chopped cucumber and fresh mint.

A Hotter Curry
for Beef, Lamb or Pork

As with the mild curry on the previous pages, you can substitute curry paste or powder for the spices listed below, or vary the spices as you like. Always make sure they are cooked well before adding the liquid – this is vital, to 'open' and mingle the spices and prevent them burning the back of your throat. The canned tomatoes can be replaced by the same quantity of plain yogurt – in which case reduce the simmering time by half.

Serves 2

1 onion, chopped
1 garlic clove, crushed
1cm piece of fresh ginger, grated
a little butter or oil for frying
2 teaspoons ground coriander
1 teaspoon ground cumin
2 teaspoons ground turmeric
a good pinch of cayenne pepper
3 cardamom pods, bruised (bash smartly with the flat side of a knife)
400g can of tomatoes, drained
2 teaspoons tomato purée
2 teacups (about 200g) diced leftover beef, lamb or pork (or fresh meat, if you prefer)
a handful of chopped fresh coriander

In a small casserole, sweat the onion, garlic and ginger in a little butter or oil until softened and beginning to colour. Add all the spices, stir well and cook over a low heat for 5 minutes. (If you are using fresh meat, add it now and turn it in the spiced oily mixture until well coated.) Stir in the tomatoes and purée, bring to the boil and then turn down the heat to a very gentle simmer. Put on the lid and cook for 30–40 minutes, until the sauce has thickened. Add the leftover meat and simmer for 5–7 minutes.

Scatter over the chopped coriander and serve with rice, mango chutney, plain yogurt or yogurt mixed with chopped cucumber and fresh mint.

You could also consider...

Root vegetable curry Omit the meat and instead add your favourite root vegetables, peeled and diced, as soon as the tomato liquid has been brought to simmering point. Potatoes and cauliflower florets are a classic (*aloo gobi*).

Paneer and pea or spinach curry Paneer (see page 206) is great with an equal quantity of frozen peas or spinach – add them to the sauce once it has begun to thicken, omitting the meat.

Jalfrezi A spicy curried dish with fresh tomatoes and green peppers, traditionally made with leftover meat. The process is the same, but add a deseeded and chopped hot green chilli to the onion mixture and replace the canned tomatoes with a similar weight of skinned and chopped fresh tomatoes and a finely sliced, deseeded green pepper. Leave out the cardamom. Simmer until the tomato sauce is thickening, then add leftover chicken or lamb.

Milder tomato curry Tame the dish by adding a teacupful of yogurt to the onion and spice mixture just before you add the tomatoes. The yogurt will reduce and thicken in the heat, coating the meat in a gorgeous satiny blanket.

Thai Curry

Making Thai curries differs from making Indian ones in a few fundamental ways. First, you are unlikely to have to make your own spice mix, since there are plenty of good Thai curry pastes on the market. Secondly, they require coconut milk, which can't really be replaced, as it can in Indian curries, with canned tomatoes or stock. Lastly, they will be immeasurably improved by the addition of a fresh lemongrass stalk, if you can get your hands on one. A final squeeze of lime juice adds a citrus edge to the creamy heat.

These are pale, fragrant and very liquid dishes, which often pack a hidden punch, though the quantity of paste I have recommended here should give you a temperate dish. There are lots of variations (see pages 87–8) and they are quick and painless to make – keep them very simple, or add the sweetness and crunch of thinly sliced red pepper or the tang of Chinese greens right at the end. Serve with boiled rice or noodles, or mix the curry and rice or noodles together in a large bowl for a one-dish supper.

As with stews and stir-fries, when you are using leftover meat you need to turn the authentic process on its head and add it at the last minute, cooking it just enough to heat through.

Serves 4

2 tablespoons vegetable oil
3–4 teaspoons Thai curry paste – red or green, as you prefer
1 tablespoon grated fresh ginger
400ml can of coconut milk
1 teaspoon grated lime zest
1 lemongrass stalk – take off the outer bark, then split and bruise
  the stalk with a rolling pin
juice of 1 lime
350g cooked chicken, roughly chopped
a good handful of fresh basil or coriander, torn into small pieces

Heat the oil in a large pan, add the curry paste and ginger and cook gently for 1–2 minutes. Slowly add the coconut milk, incorporating it well with the paste, then add the lime zest and bruised lemongrass. Reduce the heat to a very gentle simmer and cook for 5 minutes. Add the chicken and cook gently for about 5 minutes, until it is thoroughly heated through. Remove the lemongrass stalk and stir in the lime juice. Serve with the basil or coriander scattered on top and accompanied by rice – it's good with a half-and-half mix of basmati and wild rice.

You could also try...

Thai fish curry Replace the chicken with the same quantity of fish, carefully scanned for errant bones. You can add, or use on their own, 8–12 tiger prawns (usually sold raw) or 2 teacups of defrosted cooked Atlantic prawns. In either case, add 2 tablespoons of Thai fish sauce with the coconut milk. Once the liquid is simmering, add the raw tiger prawns, if using, and cook for 3–4 minutes. Then add the fish (and the cooked Atlantic prawns, if using) and cook for a further 1–2 minutes, until heated through.

Thai pork curry If you want to use pork instead of chicken, add some finely sliced spring onions with the coconut milk and a kaffir lime leaf to intensify the flavour of the lime zest.

Thai root vegetable curry Sweet potatoes and pumpkin or butternut squash (replacing the chicken) hold their shape and sweetness when poached in coconut milk and their intense orange flesh gleams brightly through it. Hard vegetables such as these, peeled and diced, will need 15–20 minutes to poach in the milk.

Thai spring or summer vegetable curry Sliced courgettes, mushrooms, peppers and mangetout all work well as substitutes for the chicken, as – unsurprisingly – do bean sprouts. The point about these is that they should retain some bite. Mangetout, mushrooms and courgettes will take 7–10 minutes to cook in the coconut milk, while very finely sliced red peppers and bean sprouts will take only a couple of minutes.

Bakes

Some of these recipes are called pies but there is no pastry here. These recipes are for bakes, with toppings such as potato, breadcrumbs or cheese – or in some cases, no topping at all. Most are quick and simple to throw together in one dish, minimising preparation time and washing up, though a few, such as shepherd's pie or fish pie, take a bit more effort. If you've got some of those round or oblong glazed terracotta dishes that are so cheap in France and Spain, this is the time to dig them out, but any ovenproof ceramic or glass dish will do just as well.

Some of the recipes that follow are brilliant ways of quickly assembling an array of ingredients from the fridge or left over from a roast, so the quantity you make will be determined by how much you have left over. Others (like those classic British potato-topped pies) cry out to be made in larger quantities than you need for one meal, since they freeze beautifully for a good three months and provide a stash of home-cooked ready meals.

Bakes are an ideal way of using up the last bits of cheese hanging around in the fridge, especially dry ends that aren't big enough to do much with. Like the last piece of bread that gets whizzed up and stored as crumbs in a box in the freezer, you could even find yourself – slightly fanatically – getting into the habit of grating all the dog-ends of hard cheeses such as Parmesan, Cheddar or red Leicester and keeping them in a jar in the fridge just for these kinds of dishes. Clearly you can't store soft or blue cheeses like this, though you'll find here several things to do with those bits, too.

Three Traditional Potato-topped Pies

Below are three very traditional British dishes that were practically invented for leftover meat. Each of them is a moveable feast insofar as you can play around with the flavours and ingredients to your heart's content.

Fish Pie

Fish pie is often overlooked as a way of using up leftovers, perhaps because we think it's going to be finicky and time-consuming to make.

Aficionados each have their particular foible – hard-boiled egg slices are either loathed or worshipped, and the presence or otherwise of tomato can cause heated debate. In fact, you can add just about anything you want: I throw in sliced leeks and/or diced carrots, or some broccoli florets, or a languishing bunch of spring onions, finely sliced and mingled with the fish. Spinach – blanched, cooled and squeezed – adds a marvellously metallic tang, softened by the white sauce. The quantities below will make just enough for a small pie for 2. Just scale up the recipe if you have plenty of fish to work with.

Serves 2

2 teaspoons butter, plus a little extra for baking
2 teaspoons plain flour
200ml milk
2 good teacups (about 250g) leftover white fish
100g frozen (cooked) prawns or shrimps, thawed
100g frozen peas
1 tablespoon chopped parsley
2 hard-boiled eggs, sliced (optional)
300g floury potatoes, peeled, boiled and mashed with a knob of butter, or 2 teacups leftover mash

Preheat the oven to 180°C/Gas Mark 4. Make a white sauce with the butter, flour and milk (see page 32). Flake the fish, checking for skin and bones, and put it in a small ovenproof dish. Add the prawns or shrimps, peas and parsley and combine with a good stir, then pour over the white sauce. If you are using hard-boiled eggs, layer the slices over the lot. Top with the mashed potato. Dot with a little butter and bake for 25–35 minutes, until bubbling and turning golden on top.

Also consider...

Smoked fish This will deepen the taste of the pie, so if you can pick up a small fillet of smoked haddock on the way home to add to leftover fish, do. Simply poach it (along with fresh white fish if you don't have leftovers) in milk with a knob of butter, allow to cool, then flake the flesh away from the skin, adding it to the rest of the fish. Keep the poaching milk to make the white sauce, giving it a much richer, fishier taste.

An enriched white sauce Replace some of the milk with single cream or crème fraîche, if you have some lying around and screaming to be used up.

A different topping Use very finely sliced raw potato instead of mash (see page 97). Or you can jazz up the mashed potato by forking through it some finely sliced leeks that have been softened in a little butter.

No-potato fish bake with fennel and capers To make a decidedly non-traditional alternative to fish pie, break the fish into large chunks in a buttered pie dish, then scatter over some sliced fennel that has been cooked in a little olive oil in a frying pan until tender and just browned. Add about a dessertspoon of well-rinsed capers and a big handful of coarsely chopped parsley, then squeeze over the juice of ½ lemon or add a drizzle of white wine. Cover with foil and bake in the oven at 180°C/ Gas Mark 4 for 15–20 minutes, until thoroughly heated through. To my taste, mashed potato doesn't sit well with the lemony capers, but a handful of breadcrumbs, mixed with a handful of grated Parmesan and toasted pine nuts and scattered over the top before baking, would provide a welcome crunch while helping to prevent the fish drying out.

No-potato fish bake with spinach Wilt a couple of large handfuls of well-washed spinach in a large pan – you need only the water that is clinging to its leaves for cooking. Once wilted, squeeze well and drape the leaves over and around large pieces of cooked white fish or salmon in a buttered baking dish. Make the white sauce as for Fish Pie, finishing off with a good handful of grated Parmesan and a grating of nutmeg – its strong flavour goes particularly well with spinach. Pour this over the dish and bake in the oven at 180°C/Gas Mark 4 for 15–20 minutes, or until just turning brown on top. Serve with some crusty bread or boiled potatoes.

No-potato fish bake with saffron, pine nuts and raisins Break the fish into large chunks and put it in a buttered dish with some chopped fresh tomatoes, a finely sliced and browned onion, a handful or so of toasted pine nuts and another of raisins. Steep a couple of strands of good saffron in ½ eggcup of hot water, then pour it over the dish. Cover with foil and bake in the oven at 180°C/Gas Mark 4 for 15 minutes.

icken Pie

ks well with any leftover meat and, as with the Fish Pie on pages
u can add whatever vegetables need using up: sweated, sliced leeks,
carrot, broccoli or cauliflower florets, French beans or even finely
sliced red or orange peppers. Adapt the basic recipe below as you like and,
if in any doubt, use the What Goes with What list on pages 26–7.

Serves 2

200ml milk
2 teacups mushrooms, sliced
2 good teacups (about 250g) leftover cooked chicken, cut into pieces
a good handful of chopped parsley
oil for frying
1 onion, chopped
1 garlic clove, crushed
2 teaspoons butter, plus a little extra for baking
2 teaspoons plain flour
a grating of nutmeg (optional)
300g floury potatoes, peeled, boiled and mashed
   with a little butter, or 2 teacups leftover mash
salt and pepper

Preheat the oven to 180°C/Gas Mark 4. Bring the milk to simmering
point in a pan, add the mushrooms and poach for 3–4 minutes, until
tender. Drain, keeping the milk to one side. Put the mushrooms and
chicken in a small ovenproof dish and scatter the parsley over it.

Heat a little oil in a small pan, add the onion and garlic and cook
gently until softened. Add to the dish containing the chicken, forking
all the ingredients together.

Make a white sauce (see page 32) using the milk from the
mushrooms and the butter and flour. Season with salt, pepper and a
grating of nutmeg, if liked. Pour this over the chicken and mushroom
mixture and stir to combine everything roughly. Spoon the mashed
potato evenly on top, smoothing it down with a fork. Dot with a little
butter and bake for 25–35 minutes, until bubbling and golden on top.

Lots more ways with chicken pie...

Mushroom sauce For a quick fix, replace the mushrooms and white sauce with half a can of mushroom soup (not the concentrated variety) or a small tub of bought mushroom sauce.

Tarragon Substituting tarragon for parsley will give a stronger, aromatic edge to the dish.

Using stock Omit the white sauce and simply spoon some home-made stock (see pages 27–30) over the meat and mushrooms before topping with mash.

Replace the mash Use very finely sliced raw potato for a Dauphinoise-style crust (see page 97).

Breadcrumb top Replace the potatoes with a crunchy layer of Flavoured Breadcrumbs (see page 49). Sprinkle this over the top of the dish, rather as you would a crumble mixture, then bake in the usual way until the topping is bubbling and browning. Serve with nutty brown rice, roasted cherry tomatoes or wilted greens.

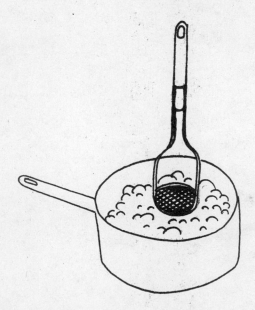

Cottage or Shepherd's Pie

My mum swears that cottage pie uses lamb and shepherd's uses beef, which seems counterintuitive to me – but the world seems divided on the issue and I don't care much either way.

I don't think I'm alone in preferring fresh meat to leftovers as a general rule in this pie – but it's still a great way of using up cooked meat, and it scores high on the granny-approval radar. Unless you have a mincer, preparation will mean a bit of careful knife work or the use of an electric chopper or food processor to pulse, so that the meat doesn't end up as a paste.

Some people like to add chopped carrot and/or celery to the meat and, frankly, you can include any vegetable you like, though I would be inclined to serve peas separately rather than adding them to the pie because they tend to toughen and lose their vibrant green.

These quantities will make a small pie for 2, so if you have much more meat available, just scale everything up.

Serves 2

a little butter or oil
1 onion, finely chopped
2 carrots, cut into small dice
1 garlic clove, crushed
200–250g leftover beef or lamb, trimmed of all fat and sinew and
   finely minced
400g can of chopped tomatoes, lightly drained of their juice.
1 tablespoon tomato purée
1 tablespoon Worcestershire sauce
300g floury potatoes, peeled, boiled and mashed with a knob of butter,
   or 2 teacups leftover mash
salt and pepper

1

Heat a little butter or oil in a pan, and add the onion, carrots and garlic. Cook gently until softened.

2

Add the meat and stir well.

3

Add the tomatoes, purée and Worcestershire sauce. Let the mixture bubble languidly for about 30 minutes, until the sauce has thickened, then season to taste. Meanwhile, preheat the oven to 200°C/Gas Mark 6.

4

Transfer the mixture to a baking dish. Top evenly with the mashed potato, dot with a little butter and bake for 20–30 minutes, until the potato is browning and the meat is bubbling.

Instead of plain mash…

Leeks Cook some finely sliced leeks in butter until softened and fork them through the mash before it goes on top of the dish.

Dauphinoise top Replace the mash with very finely sliced raw potato – a mandolin is helpful here for slicing the potato evenly. Rinse and drain the potato slices, then arrange in an overlapping layer all over the meat mixture. Season, drizzle olive oil over the potato and bake until the meat is bubbling and the potato is tender, crisping slightly on top.

Celeriac mash Use half the amount of mashed potato and mix with an equal quantity of mashed celeriac. Celeriac holds a lot of water when it is boiled, so drain it really well. It's also harder to mash smoothly – a mouli-légumes or potato ricer is handy here if you have one.

Ten Vegetable Gratins

Gratins are simply baked dishes topped with cheese – fantastic for using up any vegetables not so much left over as entering the twilight zone, plus the remnants of your favourite cheese. Once the vegetables have been softened in a steamer or with a knob of butter in a pan, they can be blanketed in a cheesy white sauce or a tomato sauce or just left in their unclothed state. In either case it's the topping that makes the dish: a grating of cheese or a cheesy breadcrumb mixture, baked until the cheese bubbles and browns or the top is crisp. This is food for cold evenings.

Cauliflower Cheese

One of my all-time favourite suppers, made with either strong Cheddar with a grating of nutmeg in the white sauce or the zingy taste of mountain cheese such as Emmental, with a pinch of mustard powder.

Serves 2

1 medium cauliflower, cut into good-sized florets
1 quantity of Cheese Sauce (see page 32), made with 1 teaspoon mustard powder
some good hard cheese for grating, or 1 teacup mixed breadcrumbs and grated cheese
bacon rashers, cut into pieces and fried until crisp, to serve (optional)

Preheat the oven to 180°C/Gas Mark 4. Put the cauliflower florets in a steamer and cook for 5–7 minutes, until just yielding to the point of a knife. Put them in an ovenproof dish and cover with the sauce, then grate some cheese over the top or scatter over the mixed breadcrumbs and cheese. Bake for 20–30 minutes, until golden and bubbling. Always ensure that the top is really golden before serving.

I like, unconventionally, to pile the cauliflower up on to a thick slice of toasted brown bread, spooning over the thick sauce and scattering pieces of bacon over the whole lot. You can, of course, serve it on its own.

Gratins to take you through the year...

Leek and parsnip Peel and dice the vegetables and either steam them or soften them in a little butter or oil in a covered saucepan. Instead of cheese sauce, cover them with double cream spiked with a good teaspoon of grainy mustard. Mature Cheddar cheese on top, with or without breadcrumbs, works beautifully. Bake as opposite.

Sweet potato, broccoli and thyme Steam the vegetables until tender and place in a dish without a cheese sauce but with a few knobs of butter, some chopped thyme and a breadcrumb topping (see page 49). Bake as opposite.

Spinach Wash plenty of spinach and then wilt it quickly in a covered pan in just the water clinging to the leaves. Drain, cool and squeeze out excess water, then put the spinach in an ovenproof dish. Pour over a white sauce seasoned with a good grating of fresh nutmeg (see page 32). If you have some ricotta cheese, crumble it over the spinach after pouring on the sauce, then finish with a plain breadcrumb topping (see page 49). Bake as opposite.

Chicory Cut the chicory heads into quarters lengthways and steam for 5 minutes. Put in a dish with some finely sliced celery and top with little knobs of Roquefort (or any blue cheese) instead of cheese sauce. Scatter over a breadcrumb and parsley topping (see page 49). Bake as opposite.

Macaroni cheese If you substitute cooked macaroni for the cauliflower you have a quite different dish. Leave out the mustard and instead stir into the sauce some Bottled Dried Tomatoes (see page 44) or bits of bacon cooked until just brown.

Celery with capers and anchovies This is an enduringly Italian combination and one of our fallbacks for the packet of celery left in the fridge. It goes really well with white meat or fish, and is equally good as a light lunch with crusty bread. Blanch 3cm-long pieces of celery in rapidly boiling salted water for 4 minutes, then drain. Put into a buttered ovenproof dish, scatter over chopped capers, garlic and anchovies to taste and drizzle with olive oil, before baking as on page 98. You could top it all off with Flavoured Breadcrumbs (see page 49).

Mushrooms with garlic and parsley Chop some mushrooms into small pieces and put them into ramekins. For each ramekin, mix in ½ clove of finely chopped garlic and a teaspoon of finely chopped parsley. Finish with a knob of butter and a sprinkling of salt and pepper, then bake as on page 98. For a gutsier alternative, add some dried chilli flakes, lemon zest, chopped thyme and a teaspoon of dry white wine per ramekin. Sprinkle more parsley on top. Serve accompanied by crusty bread or toast.

Beetroot and white sauce Boil the beetroot until soft (depending on size, this can take anything from 40 minutes upwards, and almost always takes longer than you think). Test for tenderness with a sharp knife, then drain and peel. Slice the beetroot and put it in an ovenproof dish. Add some finely sliced onion that has been cooked in a little oil or butter until soft. Make a White Sauce (see page 32), adding a bay leaf as it cooks. Season well with black pepper, pour the sauce over the beetroot and bake until bubbling. This dish is especially good with roast lamb.

Tartiflette The French Savoie equivalent of our cauliflower cheese, tartiflette makes use of boiled waxy potatoes, speckling them with ham or bacon and a coating of strong, semi-soft mountain cheese – classically, Reblochon or raclette. In some ways the dish is more a bake than a gratin, but in any case it should not be attempted by anyone with an aversion to strong, smelly cheese.

For 750g potatoes, use about 150g diced ham or browned bacon, 250g cheese and half a small pot of cream. Lightly brown some onions and garlic in butter or oil. Add the sliced boiled potatoes and let them colour gently. Arrange in an ovenproof dish, scatter over the ham or bacon (or layer the potatoes and meat, if you prefer), scatter cubes of the cheese over the top and pour over the cream. Cover with foil and bake at 180°C/Gas Mark 4 for 15–20 minutes, then remove the foil and grill for 5 minutes to give it a crisp top. For an authentic tartiflette, add chopped gherkins to the potatoes, or serve them separately.

An Arabic Bake

The Arabic name of this dish, *fatta*, means 'to break in pieces'. It is a traditional Middle Eastern dish somewhere between a bake and a warm salad (there's no oven time required), with yogurt as its essential ingredient. Although it's usually made with freshly poached meat, it works just as well with leftover chicken or lamb, the layers and textures of the dish making it particularly pleasing.

Serves 4

1 large pitta bread
60g pine nuts
675g plain yogurt
a small bunch of mint leaves, chopped
1 large garlic clove, crushed (optional)
570ml meat broth or stock (see pages 28–9) for warming the meat
4 teacups (about 400g) leftover beef, lamb or chicken, torn into pieces
400g can of chickpeas, drained

Split the pitta bread open, toast it, then leave to cool. Break into bite-sized pieces.

Warm a small frying pan over a medium heat and add the pine nuts. Toast them carefully, moving them around with a wooden spoon to make sure they do not burn. When the nuts are golden, remove them from the pan and leave to cool.

Mix the yogurt with the chopped mint and the garlic, if using. When you are almost ready to serve the dish, bring the meat broth or stock to a bare simmer in a large pan. Add the meat and chickpeas and continue to simmer for 3–5 minutes, until they are warmed through.

To assemble the dish, spread a layer of broken toasted pitta over the bottom of a deep serving dish. Remove the meat and chickpeas from the stock with a slotted spoon and arrange these over the bread. Sprinkle 4 tablespoons of the stock over the top and finally cover with the seasoned yogurt. Garnish with the toasted pine nuts and serve immediately.

Roast Vegetables

Absolutely any vegetables that are languishing in the kitchen will be transformed by this simple treatment. Roast vegetables are delicious as warm salads with green leaves and blue cheese, goat's cheese or Parmesan (see pages 210–11). They can form a rich body for soup, luxuriantly sweetening it with their caramel flavour (see pages 56–63); or they can just be tossed with pasta, rice or couscous, used in a vegetarian lasagne or served as a side dish. Roast root vegetables are particularly delicious served with couscous and a little harissa thinned with olive oil to make a dressing.

Preheat the oven to 200°C/Gas Mark 6. Peel and/or deseed the vegetables as appropriate and cut into large chunks. Arrange in a roasting tin in a single layer, sprinkle olive oil over them and toss well so that they are evenly coated in the oil. Season lightly, then place the tin on the highest shelf of the oven and roast for 30–40 minutes, until tender and golden, turning half way through (or giving them a good shake).

Candidates for roasting ...

Aubergines Lovely cut in half lengthways and baked with a drizzle of olive oil and a good pinch of dried chilli flakes. To serve, scatter some slightly salty feta or milder ricotta cheese and chopped mint on top, along with a squeeze of lemon. Eat hot or cold.

Asparagus Will not take very long to roast in a hot oven just coated in olive oil. Serve with crisp bacon.

Sweet potatoes Cut lengthways into quarters, drizzle with oil, season with salt and pepper and toss with a little fresh thyme if you have it. Roast the potatoes until meltingly tender. Serve with crumbled goat's cheese and toasted pine nuts, plus a peppery rocket or watercress salad.

Sweet or ordinary potatoes Delicious cut into chunks, drizzled with olive oil and roasted with crushed garlic, quartered lemons and a pinch of good paprika. You could also add some thyme and chunks of red onion. Serve warm with crumbled feta cheese.

Trimmed whole leeks or celery Roast as described opposite, then scatter lots of grated Parmesan over them and return to the oven for 5 minutes before serving.

Peppers, tomatoes and anchovies Stuff halved, deseeded peppers with chopped tomatoes or halved cherry tomatoes. Scatter a little crushed garlic, a couple of chopped anchovy fillets and some ground black pepper over the top, then drizzle with olive oil. Roast until the filling has turned to a slight mush and the peppers are soft. Scatter basil on top and serve with crusty bread, rice or couscous.

Parsnips and carrots To counter their sweetness, scatter over a few fennel seeds before roasting. Serve at room temperature on a green herb salad with a splash of oil and lemon juice. Use any leftovers mashed in a soup.

Pumpkin or squash Roast with some whole unpeeled garlic cloves, a pinch of dried chilli flakes and a drizzle of oil. Serve with green leaves and scatter toasted sesame or poppy seeds on top, or mash on to crusty bread – with a mild goat's cheese, if you like it. The garlic cloves will roast sweetly inside their papery skin, which will fall off easily once they are cooked. You don't eat the skin!

Courgettes Roast as described opposite until stickily sweet and golden, then serve with toasted pine nuts.

Beetroot Something wonderful happens to beetroot when they are roasted. Scrub the beetroot and trim the roots before roasting whole (they may take up to an hour in the oven, depending on their size). You don't need to peel them – the skin will fall away when they are cooked. Use in soups, salads or risotto or serve as a warm salad with Puy lentils and goat's cheese.

Two Spiced Lamb Bakes

Here are two dishes from Greece and Africa that are alike in kind but have their own particular character. Depending on how much leftover lamb you have, either recipe can easily be halved or scaled up. Don't be put off by the fairly lengthy ingredients lists either – most of them are basic store-cupboard things.

Leftover-lamb Moussaka

If your view of moussaka is that it is an over-oily and oddly orange concoction, I'd love to change your mind. Part of the problem can be that aubergines are notoriously thirsty for oil, so be strict with them and don't go on adding more oil if they look dry when you are frying them. Once they start to brown on both sides, they release most of the oil they've sucked up and can then be drained on kitchen paper. Alternatively – and this is what I do – you can brush them with a very little oil and bake or grill them instead of frying, turning half way through to ensure they are golden on both sides. Raw minced lamb would also add to the oily situation if you were using it. Leftover lamb, of course, has already lost its fat so, actually, it's ideal.

Serves 2

1 aubergine, cut into slices about 5mm thick
olive oil
1 onion, thinly sliced
1 garlic clove, crushed
400g can of chopped tomatoes, drained of their juice
1 tablespoon tomato purée
1 small glass of red wine
1 bay leaf
1 scant teaspoon ground cinnamon
2 teacups (about 200g) leftover cooked lamb,
   minced or finely chopped

104

2 teaspoons butter
2 teaspoons plain flour
200ml milk
20g strong hard cheese, such as Cheddar, Parmesan or Gruyère, grated
1 egg
a grating of nutmeg
salt and pepper

Brush the aubergine slices with olive oil and then grill them (or bake them at 180°C/Gas Mark 4) until golden on both sides, turning once. Remove from the oven and leave to cool.

Heat a little olive oil in a saucepan, add the onion and garlic and cook gently until softened. Stir in the tomatoes, tomato purée, wine, bay leaf and cinnamon. Bring to the boil, then turn down the heat and very gently simmer for about 20 minutes, until thickened. Stir in the meat and heat through.

Make a cheese sauce with the butter, flour, milk and cheese according to the instructions on page 32, then leave to cool. Whisk the egg in a separate bowl and add it to the cooled sauce, whisking as you go. Season with salt, pepper and nutmeg.

To assemble the dish, put half the meat mixture in an ovenproof dish and cover with half the aubergines. Repeat with the rest of the meat and aubergines. Pour the eggy, cheesy sauce on top and then bake at 180°C/Gas Mark 4 for 25–30 minutes, until the top is golden. Serve with rice or crusty bread and a crisp salad.

Bobotie

Bobotie comes from South Africa. With its eggy, milky heart, it's a mildly curried relative of moussaka, but without the aubergines. I love to serve it with a mixture of finely chopped tomato and onion as a relish, and yellow turmeric rice dotted with a handful of raisins.

Serves 4

1 large slice of bread
250ml milk
25g butter
1 dessert apple, peeled, cored and chopped
1 large onion, finely chopped
2 garlic cloves, chopped
½ teaspoon curry powder
4 teacups (about 400g) leftover cooked lamb,
  minced or finely chopped
3 tablespoons mango chutney (or any other chutney)
1 tablespoon chopped or flaked almonds
1 tablespoon raisins
a good grating of nutmeg
2 bay leaves
1 tablespoon lemon juice
3 eggs
salt and pepper

Preheat the oven to 180°C/Gas Mark 4. Soak the bread in the milk. Squeeze it out and reserve both, separately. Melt the butter in a frying pan, add the apple, onion and garlic and cook gently until soft. Stir in the curry powder and cook for 1 minute.

Put the meat in a bowl with the squeezed-out bread, chutney, almonds, raisins, nutmeg, bay leaves and lemon juice, then add the curried onion mixture. Mix the whole lot together and season with salt and pepper. Put the mixture into a buttered ovenproof dish and press down. Then mix the eggs with the milk from the soaked bread and pour them over the meat. Bake for about 30 minutes, until the topping is set and lightly golden.

Pies, Tarts
and Pizzas

Pies have long been part of the rhythm of using up cooked meat and heaps of ripening fruit, but nowadays we tend to think of them as difficult to make. It's just not true, especially if you use bought pastry. This is leftovers, after all, the kind of cooking that is meant to be as relaxed and effortless as possible. Keep a packet of good frozen pastry in the freezer – one of the kinds that use real butter rather than transfats and hydrogenated oils – and you just have to remember to defrost it a few hours before you actually need it. The rest is a satisfying doddle: decide on the shape you want, make a filling with a little juicy sauce and close it all up. Once a pie is brushed with egg yolk and baked, it *always* looks beautiful, resonating with domestic competence.

Somewhere between pastry and bread, pizza dough is simple stuff to make too. There's no reason to be frightened of yeast, which comes in packets and just gets on with the job once activated with liquid and warmth. If you have one, use a bread-making machine, or you could buy pizza bases (but they tend to be chemical-rich) or use a baguette as your base. Whichever you go for, pizzas are the ultimate convenience food, and very hands-on. Let everyone choose what they want on theirs from an array of leftovers or vegetables that have to be used up fast.

Pastry

If you decide to make your own shortcrust pastry, which you can also freeze for later, this recipe can be used for virtually all the sweet and savoury pies and tarts that follow. It has a light, crumbly texture and is not complicated to make.

Bear in mind that pastry is one of those things that require precision and light-handedness, so don't be inventive with the quantities, and don't over handle it. Work briskly and try to keep everything as cool as possible, using only the tips of your fingers (the coldest part of your hands). If your hands are hot, run them under the cold tap and then dry them before making the pastry. If the oven is on, work as far away from it as you can.

There's no great magic to rolling pastry, save for the caveat that you should handle it as little as possible. Work fairly swiftly, with an even, gentle pressure on the rolling pin, having dusted both the clean work surface and your rolling pin with a bit of plain flour to prevent the pastry sticking to them – and you will need to re-dust them as you go. You don't need to turn the pastry over as you roll it; a quarter turn between each rolling will keep it in a roughly even shape.

You'll find the basic shortcrust pastry recipe overleaf, with ideas for all the things that you can make with it (and blind baking instructions) on pages 112–13.

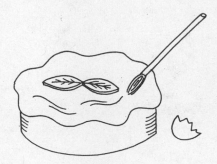

Shortcrust Pastry

If you have lard, you can substitute it for half the butter when making savoury pies, but always **use butter for sweet ones.** And don't throw out your pastry trimmings – re-shape them into a ball and roll out to make jam tarts, mince pies or cheese straws (see pages 112–13).

220g plain flour
a pinch of salt
110g unsalted butter, at room temperature but not too soft
about 2½–3 tablespoons chilled water

1
Sift the flour into a bowl with the salt.

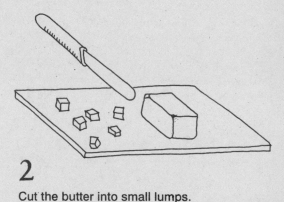

2
Cut the butter into small lumps.

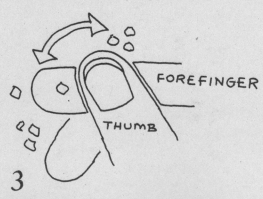

3
Rub the butter into the flour, using your fingertips ...

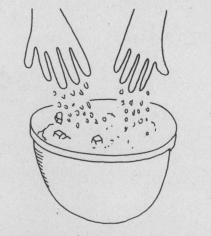

4
... and lifting the mixture up to get as much air into it as possible. Stop as soon as you have a fine mixture that resembles breadcrumbs.

5

Add the water very slowly and evenly, mixing as you go with a round-bladed knife or a spatula and finally with your hands, until you have a ball of pliable dough that just holds together.

6

Wrap the pastry in cling film and leave it in the fridge to relax for at least half an hour.

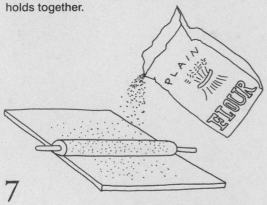

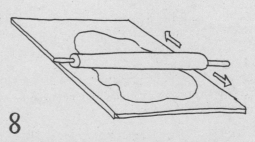

7

To roll out the pastry, dust both the clean work surface and your rolling pin with a little flour.

8

Use an even, gentle pressure on the rolling pin, rolling until the pastry is about 3–5mm thick. Chill the pastry in the fridge for at least 20 minutes before filling.

Crucial tips

- Whatever kind of filling you choose, be it meat, fish, vegetable or fruit, pies come in all shapes and sizes. In every case you should let the pastry rest in the fridge for 20 minutes or so before filling it – this should prevent it shrinking during the cooking time.
- It is really important to make sure the filling is cool before using it, so it is useful to make the filling first, allowing it time to cool while you roll and rest the pastry.
- Once you have covered a pie with pastry, brush the top with beaten egg or – easier – milk to make it shiny and golden when it emerges from the oven.

What you can do with pastry...

Any of the pie filling recipes and variations on pages 115–19 can be made up into different kinds of 'pie', according to what you like the look of:

Pasties The simplest, no-pot pie is a pastry envelope in the shape of a Cornish pasty or half-moon. It's like scrunching up a rather badly wrapped parcel and whatever you do it can't fail to look amazing. For a pasty big enough to serve 2, roll out the pastry to a rectangle roughly 30 x 20cm and about 3–5mm thick. Transfer this to a lightly greased baking tray and let it rest in the fridge for about 20 minutes. Plonk the (cooled) filling into the centre and draw up the longest sides over the top until they meet in the middle. Then pinch and squash the edges together until you get to each end. Curl these 'tails' around, squash them down and cut off any excess.

For individual pasties, cut out pastry circles about 15cm in diameter, fill them, fold them in half to form a half-moon shape and then lightly push down all around the edges to seal.

Bake at 200°C/Gas Mark 6 until crisp and golden.

One-crust pies Fill a pie dish half full. For a large pie, place an upside-down eggcup or a pie funnel in the middle of the dish to help support the pastry lid. Then roll out the pastry to about 3–5mm thick and cut a ribbon from round the edge to fit the rim of the dish. Dampen the rim with a little water and press the pastry ribbon on to it, trimming to fit if necessary. Brush this pastry edge with water, then cut out a pastry top slightly wider than you need, place it over the pie and press it down firmly on to the pastry below it, using your fingers or the blade of a blunt knife. Trim off any excess pastry. Make a small cut in the top of the pastry to let the steam out. I use leftover pastry to make decorations of flowers or leaves – just brush them underneath with milk or egg and stick them to the pastry lid. Then brush milk or egg all over the pie to give it a shiny golden crust once baked. Bake at 200°C/Gas Mark 6 until crisp and golden.

Tarts Roll out the pastry to 3–5mm thick, then lift it up on the rolling pin and gently fit it into a tart tin or ceramic flan case, pushing it into the edges and making sure no air is trapped inside. Let it rest in the fridge for 20 minutes or so. Preheat the oven to 200°C/Gas Mark 6. Trim off the overlapping pastry, then prick the base all over with a fork. Line the base and sides with a sheet of baking parchment and fill with baking beans, or with ordinary dried beans or rice, to bake 'blind'. Bake for 12–15 minutes, until the paper will lift off the pastry easily. Return to the oven without the paper and beans for about 5 minutes longer, until the pastry is lightly golden. Leave to cool before adding the filling.

You can also use spare pastry trimmings to make jam tarts or mince pies. Squish the trimmings into a ball and roll out. Cut into rounds slightly larger than the holes in your tart tin and gently press them in. Add a level teaspoon of jam or mincemeat and bake in an oven preheated to 200°C/Gas Mark 6 for 7–10 minutes.

No-tin tarts for fruit Puff pastry, cut into one large or several smaller rectangles, is brilliant for making simple fruit tarts or *galettes*. Roll the pastry out to 3–5mm thick, then trim the sides to make a rectangle. Place on a baking sheet. With a sharp knife, score a line 1cm inside each edge to make a border, then either simply spread jam on the pastry or just top it with sliced fruit and scatter over some sugar, being sure to keep the filling within the border. Bake at 200°C/Gas Mark 6 for 10–15 minutes, until puffed and golden.

Filo pastry Available in frozen packs, sheets of filo pastry are essential for making Greek or Middle Eastern pies such as the filo pie on page 123, but could also be used for any of the recipes in this section. Filo needs to be brushed with oil or melted butter before use to prevent it drying out. Since it is so fragile, you need to work fairly quickly or it will become brittle. Keep the stack of pastry sheets under a clean, damp cloth, taking out one sheet at a time to layer into your dish. As a general rule, you will need two or three layers for the base and top of any pie.

Cheese straws Puff pastry is best for cheese straws. Roll out the pastry and grate some fairly strong Cheddar or Gloucester cheese on top of it. Fold the pastry in half and roll it out again. If you want very cheesy straws, you can repeat the process. Otherwise cut the cheesy pastry into strips around 7.5 x 2.5cm. Brush with milk or beaten egg and bake in an oven preheated to 200°C/Gas Mark 6 for 7–10 minutes, until golden.

A Straightforward Chicken Pie –
with Masses of Variations

With pie fillings, you need to remember that leftover meat is short on juices so you will always have to add a little liquid – anything from wine to cream or stock. Let it simmer in the pan so that it reduces a little and you shouldn't need any flour for thickening. I find it easiest and quickest to make all my pie fillings in a frying pan, and I prefer to leave creamy white and cheese sauces (see page 32) for bakes – though they do work brilliantly with leftover meat in vol au vents.

This recipe uses chicken but there are endless variations for making fillings with other leftover meat or vegetables. Almost all of them start with an onion and garlic base and, because the pastry itself is quite filling, you won't need a great mound of meat or vegetables: a good rule of thumb is to allow about a teacupful of trimmed leftover meat per person. Work with what you have, and bulk it up with vegetables if you think you need more. You could turn any of these pie fillings into a baked dish by replacing the pastry with a top layer of herby breadcrumbs or mashed potato (see pages 94–5).

Serves 2

oil or butter for frying
1 onion, finely chopped
1 garlic clove, finely chopped
1 teacup mushrooms, sliced
about 1 teacup leftover vegetables, chopped small: potatoes, carrots,
     leeks, fennel and French beans are all good with chicken
a small glass of white wine or vermouth (or stock, if you prefer)
a squeeze of lemon juice
1 teaspoon Dijon mustard
2 teaspoons chopped thyme or parsley

1 teacup (about 100g) leftover chicken (or other poultry), torn into
  strips or chunks
2–4 tablespoons cream (this is one occasion when those single cubes
  of frozen leftover cream come in extremely handy – see page 21)
½ quantity of Shortcrust Pastry (see pages 110–11) if making a pie,
  1 quantity of Shortcrust Pastry if making a pasty – or use 200g or
  400g bought pastry respectively
a little beaten egg, or milk, for brushing
salt and pepper

Heat some oil or butter in a large frying pan, add the onion and garlic
and cook gently until softened but not coloured.

Add the mushrooms and cook until they are tender and the liquid
has reduced. Stir in the vegetables and cook for a minute or two.

Add the wine/vermouth or stock and the lemon juice and let it
bubble for a minute or two, until slightly reduced. You can add more
liquid if things are looking a bit too syrupy. Stir in the mustard and the
thyme or parsley, then season to taste. Stir in the meat and enough
cream to make the mixture moistly sloppy without being runny. Leave
to cool completely.

Preheat the oven to 200°C/Gas Mark 6. Roll out the pastry and use
to make a pie or pasty, as described on page 112. Brush the pastry with
egg or milk. Bake for 30–40 minutes, until crisp and golden.

Serve with a salad or, alternatively, with some shredded cabbage that
has been boiled until just tender, then drained and tossed in a frying pan
in hot olive oil with a good pinch of dried chilli flakes.

Lots of pie fillings...

These are suggestions for delicious flavour combinations but of course
this is about using up what you have around, so there is no need to
stick rigidly to the ideas – particularly when it comes to which vegetables
you choose.

Chicken, bacon and leek Brown some chopped bacon and use a finely
sliced leek instead of onion. Proceed as above but substitute cream for
the wine/stock and omit the vegetables and mushrooms.

More pie fillings...

Turkey and ham A perfect Christmas leftover pie. Substitute turkey and ham for the chicken. You could also add diced leftover roast vegetables, plus a couple of teaspoons of cranberry sauce or redcurrant jelly for a slightly sweet, syrupy sauce. Fresh tarragon tastes lovely with turkey.

Turkey and mascarpone This is good for quite a quantity of meat so works better as a pie than a pasty. First sauté some leeks and mushrooms in a little oil until tender, then add the meat. Season with salt, pepper and mustard. Add a small tub of mascarpone or bought mushroom sauce and heat through. Any raw or cooked vegetables can be added, such as broccoli, carrots or beans – if they are raw, make sure they are diced small enough to cook in the time it takes for the pie to be ready.

Poultry with Middle Eastern spices Season the softened onion with a good pinch each of ground ginger, allspice and cinnamon, adding a couple of strands of saffron, if you have it. Leave to cool for 5 minutes, then stir in the meat. Instead of adding stock or wine, fork in a lightly beaten egg, a teaspoon of butter and a handful of finely chopped parsley. The egg should not become scrambled but just coat the other ingredients. This would be especially nice made with filo pastry (see page 113).

Pheasant or other game Substitute leftover cooked game for the chicken. Add sliced leeks and/or mushrooms to the onion base and proceed as on the previous page but, instead of adding wine and lemon juice, make a little gravy with a teaspoon of Dijon mustard, a dash of Worcestershire sauce and a wineglass or so of stock.

Shredded roast duck Duck is lovely mixed with a little browned pancetta or a handful of chopped cooked bacon and some potatoes (either diced leftover cooked ones or raw potatoes, peeled and diced very small, so that they cook properly). If you have some Marsala, remove the duck mixture from the pan once it is cooked, return the pan to the heat and add a good slug of Marsala. Let it bubble away for a minute while you stir with a wooden spoon to scrape up any bits that have stuck to the bottom of the pan. Mix this syrupy liquid into your pie filling.

Pork with sharp apples Once the onion has softened, add a peeled, cored and finely diced apple. To make the sauce, use a big teaspoon of Dijon mustard, a scattering of chopped tarragon in place of the thyme or parsley and vermouth rather than wine or stock. Let it bubble away for a good 30 seconds to reduce slightly and thicken, then stir in the pork.

Pork with mushrooms Proceed as for the main recipe, substituting pork for the chicken and cream for the wine or stock. Pork and mushrooms on their own are quite delicious. As with other variations, though, add what you have to hand: finely sliced and softened fennel or red cabbage would be particularly good with this too.

Pork with parsnips Leftover roast parsnips will give a real sweetness to this pie – alternatively, use a peeled and finely diced raw parsnip.

Ham and cheese This works best as a pasty and is a great way of using up the end of a boiled ham. Once the chopped onion and garlic have been cooked, put them in a bowl with diced or torn ham. For an Italian-style dish add a good handful of grated Parmesan and a ball of mozzarella, cut into pieces. Fork in an egg and stir until the mixture becomes richly creamy. Season and add a tablespoon or so of fresh herbs – basil, chives or parsley would be nice. The mixture, as always, should be moist without being sloppy.

Beef and butterbeans (or root vegetables such as potatoes, parsnips and turnips) Substitute beef for the chicken and replace the mushrooms with canned butterbeans or root vegetables. If the vegetables are raw, cut them into small dice and soften with the onion, then add the meat and heat through. Use a few strips of Bottled Roasted Peppers (see page 44) for sweetness and texture and some Bottled Dried Tomatoes (see page 44) or skinned diced fresh tomatoes, adding a wineglass or so of stock if the mixture looks too dry.

More pie fillings...

Steak and mushroom It's rare to have any leftover steak but if you do, this is a classic British pie. First brown a small handful of lardons or chopped bacon with the onion (or, even better, replace the onion with tiny whole peeled shallots just browned in oil). Add some raw kidneys, in small dice, if you like them, and then the leftover meat. Add a small glass of red wine and let it bubble for a couple of minutes. Finish with a dash of Worcestershire sauce.

Lamb and potatoes Follow the main recipe, substituting lamb for the chicken and using either white or sweet potatoes, plus carrots, chopped oregano and parsley.

Tunisian filo pie with beef, lamb or dark poultry meat Add some drained canned white beans, ground black pepper, a good pinch of ground cinnamon and a couple of strands of saffron to the softened onion. When they are warmed through, transfer to a bowl and add the shredded or diced meat. Break an egg into the mixture and mix with a fork until creamy. Brush sheets of filo with oil and make a pie in a small roasting dish, using 2 sheets of oiled pastry for the base, then adding the filling in the middle and a top layer of 2 further sheets of oiled filo. Prick lightly with a fork, brush with egg and bake as normal.

White fish Use finely sliced leek instead of the onion and soften gently in butter rather than oil. Add diced raw potatoes and cook until softened (or use leftover potatoes, in which case they need no further cooking). Add the fish, along with a handful of defrosted cooked prawns if you have some to hand, and the crumbled or grated ends of a hard cheese such as Lancashire or Cheddar. Stir in some chopped parsley or chives.

Cheese Filo pastry is an ideal medium for using up the ends of cheese, and pasties work well with this type of filling too. Cottage Cheese or Paneer (see page 206), Parmesan, mozzarella, goat's cheese and hard cheeses will all be fine on their own or in combination. Cook the onion and garlic as for the main recipe and then leave to cool. Add about a teacup of cheese (grated or broken into small pieces) and some chopped chives or other herbs. Mix in an egg, then either wrap the mixture in oiled filo pastry sheets or make it into a pasty with shortcrust pastry. Bake as on pages 114–15.

Vegetables and cheese Use either leftover cooked vegetables or lightly steamed, finely chopped raw vegetables. Cook the onion and garlic as in the main recipe, then add the vegetables and a roughly equal volume of grated cheese. Moisten the mixture with a little crème fraîche, stock or a beaten egg, then add herbs of choice. Lovely partnerships include broccoli or endive with crumbled blue cheese; parsnips and grated Parmesan; sweet potato, crumbled goat's cheese and thyme; leeks, pumpkin, broccoli and grated Cheddar; spinach and Paneer (see page 206), Parmesan or ricotta.

Tourte berrichonne Traditionally this is a double-crust potato and bacon pie, but the filling ingredients work brilliantly together in any kind of pastry and are lovely in a pasty. Cook some onion and garlic until softened, then add a teacupful or so of small cubes of raw potato or larger chunks of leftover cooked potato, along with a good handful of cooked chopped bacon and a tablespoon of chopped flat-leaf parsley. The Italian version of this pie includes finely sliced leeks, chopped tomatoes, capers and olives.

Mushrooms, garlic and bacon Another wonderful combination. Cook the onion and garlic (using an extra garlic clove) until softened, then add some chopped bacon and fry lightly. Add sliced large mushrooms or whole small button mushrooms and cook until they are softened and the juices have reduced. Add a splash of white wine, let it bubble for a minute or so, then stir in about a tablespoon of single cream and some chopped parsley.

Savoury Tarts

With pastry, a couple of eggs and some cream, vegetables that need using up are easily transformed into simple tarts, as is a handful of leftover meat. The amount of effort you make is up to you. For speed, you could use a bought pastry case or, if you want to use your own or frozen pastry, follow the instructions for baking pastry cases blind on page 113.

An Onion Tart

An easy variation on traditional quiche, easily adaptable for almost any kind of leftovers or vegetables.

Serves 4

1 quantity of Shortcrust Pastry (see pages 110–11)
  or a bought 20cm pastry case
2 tablespoons olive oil
3 onions – or, better, 1 red, 1 white, 2 shallots and a
  bunch of spring onions – finely chopped
a handful of chopped sage (optional)
2 eggs
300ml crème fraîche or soured cream
  (or whole milk as a thrifty alternative)
salt and pepper

Roll out the pastry and use to line a 20cm flan tin, then bake it blind (see page 113). Leave to cool while you make the filling.

Preheat the oven to 180°C/Gas Mark 4. For the filling, heat the oil in a pan, add the onions and cook gently until soft and translucent. Leave to cool, then stir in the sage, if using. Put the mixture in the pastry case. Lightly whisk the eggs with the crème fraîche or soured cream (or milk) and season with salt and pepper. Pour this mixture over the onions and bake for about 30 minutes, until the top of the tart is bouncy to the touch and golden brown.

Using only one onion as the base, you could also try...

Cheese and bacon Add a teacup of grated hard cheese and lightly cooked bacon pieces to the cooked onion. A heaped teaspoon of Dijon mustard would go well here, whisked into the eggs and cream.

Chicken and bacon Add a good handful of leftover shredded chicken and a couple of rashers of diced lightly cooked bacon to the cooked onion (or use a sliced leek instead of the onion). Stir some fresh thyme or finely chopped parsley into the eggs and cream.

Ham and sweetcorn Add a teacup of diced cooked ham and ½ teacup of cooked sweetcorn to the cooked onion. You could also add a good handful of grated hard cheese. Add the eggs and cream, with a teaspoon of Dijon mustard, if you like, and proceed as opposite.

Sausages Use up cooked sausages by dicing them over the base of softened onion (or a layer of Onion Marmalade, see page 42), before adding the eggs and cream. If you happen to have some black pudding left over, then use that – it's particularly delicious with some sliced cooked fennel.

Sweet potato, broccoli and sage Peel 1 large or 2 small sweet potatoes and dice into small pieces. Cut some broccoli into small florets (if you would prefer to use larger florets, lightly steam them and leave to cool). Cook the sweet potato in oil or butter with a sliced onion until tender, then leave to cool. Put into the tart case with the broccoli, scatter chopped sage on top and then add the egg and cream filling as above. Use thyme if you can't get sage.

Pumpkin, leek and feta cheese (or Brie) Substitute a finely sliced leek for the onion, cooking it in a little butter or oil with 2–3 teacups of peeled diced pumpkin flesh. When the pumpkin is tender, leave to cool, then place in the pastry case. Crumble over some feta cheese (or add some slices of Brie), then pour in the eggs and cream and bake as opposite.

More savoury tarts using only one onion as the base...

Leek or fennel Omit the onion for this. Finely sliced leeks or fennel are lovely just on their own with grated Cheddar cheese. Cook them first in butter until soft, then place in the pastry case, cover with the egg and cream mixture and bake as in the main recipe on page 120.

Spinach and lamb Substitute spring onions for the onion base. Blanch, drain and squeeze out 3 or 4 large handfuls of spinach, then leave to cool. Put the spinach in the tart case, tear in some pieces of leftover lamb with some chopped mint and a good grinding of black pepper. Add the eggs and cream and bake as in the main recipe on page 120.

Tomato, basil and goat's cheese Particularly good for gluts of tiny tomatoes. Simply cut them in half and scatter them over a layer of softened onion in the pastry case. Toss in some torn basil leaves and crumble over a small goat's cheese, before adding the eggs and cream and baking as in the main recipe on page 120.

Vegetables and cheese Many of the vegetable and cheese combinations for vegetable gratins on pages 99–100 work really well here: endive and blue cheese or spinach and ricotta (or Gruyère), for example. Or try artichoke hearts and ricotta; leek and Cheddar; or courgettes or aubergines with goat's cheese or ricotta. Slice the vegetables and cook them in a little butter or oil until softened (if using courgettes or aubergines, let them brown a little and then drain well on kitchen paper before adding to the pastry case). Put them in the pastry case and crumble over the cheese. If you have a slice or two of prosciutto, tear it up over the vegetables before adding the eggs and cream and baking as in the main recipe on page 120.

Smoked fish and Parmesan Odd though it sounds, this is a delicious way of using up any fish left over from a fish pie or a kipper breakfast. Flake the fish into the pastry case, on top of the onion. Add a handful of grated Parmesan, lots of chopped chives and a small grating of nutmeg, then add the eggs and cream and bake as in the main recipe on page 120.

A Filo Pie

Spanakopita is traditionally made in Greece with spinach. However, I've found Sarah Raven's recipe in her *Garden Cookbook* (Bloomsbury Publishing, 2007) for an alternative using grated courgettes so lip-smackingly useful during summer's courgette glut that I've adapted it here. The technique is the same whatever filling you use.

This is such a warm-weather pie that it is at its best served at room temperature. It's ideal for picnics, holding its shape beautifully once cold and sliced.

Serves 4–6

1kg courgettes
olive oil
1 onion, finely chopped
2 medium eggs
4 tablespoons double cream
melted butter (or oil) for brushing
6 sheets of filo pastry
170g feta cheese, broken into rough lumps
a bunch of spring onions, chopped
a handful each of chopped flat-leaf parsley and mint
  (add some dill, if you like)
salt and pepper

Grate the courgettes, salt them well and allow to drain in a colander over the sink for about 20 minutes. Then rinse well and squeeze out excess water. Lightly cook the courgettes in a frying pan in a little olive oil until they are just colouring and any liquid has evaporated, then leave to cool.

Heat a little oil in a small pan, add the onion and cook gently until softened but not coloured. Remove from the heat and leave to cool.

Preheat the oven to 200°C/Gas Mark 6. Lightly whisk the eggs in a separate bowl, then whisk in the cream, followed by the cooked onion and some salt and pepper.

Brush a baking tin about 20cm square with melted butter or oil. Take one filo sheet, covering the remaining ones with a damp tea towel, and brush it on one side with melted butter or oil. Drape it over the base of the tin and up the sides, then repeat with 2 more sheets, laying them on top of the first one. Make sure there are no gaps and that the pastry edges flop out over the sides of the tin.

Spread the courgettes and feta cheese over the pastry. Pour over the egg and cream mixture, scatter over the chopped spring onions and herbs and fork them in lightly. Then flip over the edges of the filo pastry. Brush the remaining sheets with butter or oil, layer them over the top of the pie and tuck the edges well down into the sides of the dish. Drizzle the top with a little olive oil or melted butter and prick it all over with a fork.

Bake for 30–40 minutes, until the pastry is golden. Leave to cool in its tin, covered with a clean tea towel, and serve when just slightly warm or at room temperature.

Try out some other fillings...

Spinach Wash 1kg spinach, then put it in a large saucepan with only the water that clings to its leaves. Cook over a high heat, stirring constantly, for 2–3 minutes, until the leaves have wilted to a mere fraction of their original size. Allow to cool, then squeeze out well and chop finely (if you are using baby leaf spinach, you will not need to chop it). Spread it over the pastry with the feta and then proceed as in the main recipe.

Leftover chicken Add some cooked chicken, shredded fairly small, to the filling. In this case you could use either courgettes or spinach, or use the same quantity of leeks, sliced finely and cooked in butter until soft.

Leftover lamb Add some finely chopped or torn leftover lamb to either courgettes or spinach and omit the feta, adding extra parsley and even some chopped tomatoes, if you like.

Swiss chard Another lovely alternative. Strip the leaves from the thickest part of the stalks and shred them roughly. Slice the stalks separately and cook in a little oil until softened. Stir in the leaves and cook until

124

wilted. Add a handful of toasted pine nuts and the zest of ½ lemon to the filling.

Beef or lamb, rice and feta cheese To make a small pie for 2, soften a diced onion and a crushed garlic clove in a little butter in a pan, add a chopped large tomato, a tablespoon or so of risotto rice and a couple of teacups of diced cooked beef or lamb. Combine well. Add 2 tablespoons of water or stock, a pinch of ground cinnamon and a grinding of pepper. Cook until the rice is *al dente*, topping up the liquid if necessary. Allow to cool. Spread the mixture into a small pie dish lined with filo pastry. Mix together an egg and a tablespoon of crumbled feta cheese and pour over the meat. Cover with more filo and bake as in the main recipe.

Pizzas

Pizza dough is dead simple to make and pizzas are not something to be scared of. Effectively, they are leftovers on toasted dough, limited only by your imagination or what you have hanging around in the fridge or vegetable basket – and they take only minutes to cook.

The trick is to get the oven as hot as you can and to use a metal or terracotta base that heats really efficiently. A pizza stone is good; a baking tray is fine but works less well; an upturned roasting tin is worth considering too. Though it is clunky, I often make small pizzas by lightly oiling the underneath of a big cast iron casserole, putting it in the oven upside down and getting it really hot, then using the base to cook the dough.

Classic Italian Pizza

You can make things really simple if you have a bread maker, by using the most basic recipe for white bread and setting the machine on its 'dough only' setting. Most Italian pizza cooks swear that adding a bit of dough from a previous batch gives freshly made dough a deeper, nuttier taste, so if you do have some left over, cover it tightly with cling film to seal out any air and keep it in the fridge for up to a week. If you want to keep it for longer, pizza dough freezes well.

Enough for four 25cm pizzas

a double quantity of Quick Tomato Sauce (see page 36)
mozzarella and/or grated hard cheese

For the dough:
500g strong white flour
1 sachet (7g) easy-bake yeast
1 teaspoon salt
300ml tepid water
1 tablespoon olive oil

1

First make the dough. Sift the flour into a bowl, add the yeast and salt and stir to combine.

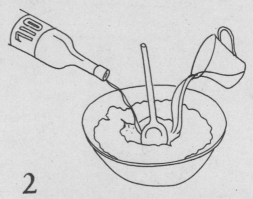

2

Make a well in the centre and gradually add the water and oil, stirring until the ingredients come together in a dough that pulls away from the side of the bowl easily; you may need a little more or less water, depending on the absorbency of the flour.

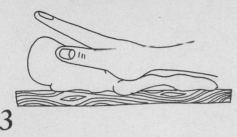

3

Turn the dough out on to a lightly floured surface and knead for 5–10 minutes by pushing it away from you with the heel of one hand and pulling the far edge over on top of itself with the other, giving it a quarter turn every now and then.

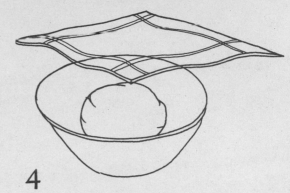

4

When the dough feels smooth and springy, shape it into a ball and place in a clean bowl. Cover with a cloth and leave in a warm place for about an hour, until doubled in volume.

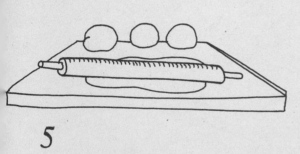

5

Once again, knead the dough on a lightly floured surface – but this time for only a few minutes, until you have punched a good bit of the air out of it. Then divide into 4 balls (or 8 if you want small pizzas) and roll each one out into a rough circle around 3mm thick, using a rolling pin or a combination of rolling and stretching by hand.

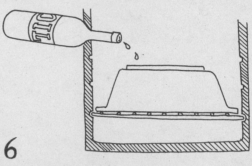

6

Preheat the oven to the hottest it will go. If you are cooking the pizza on the base of a cast iron casserole dish (see page 125), turn the dish upside down, lightly oil the base and leave it in the oven to preheat. (Alternatively, use a pizza stone or an upturned baking tray in place of the casserole dish.)

7

Spread the tomato sauce quite thinly over the dough bases, finishing with slices of mozzarella and/or grated cheese.

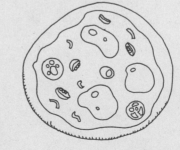

8

Place the pizza on the upturned casserole dish and bake for 7–15 minutes, according to the thickness of the base, until the base is cooked and crisp and the edges are browning.

A host of pizza ideas...

The ends of hard cheese Spread the pizza bases with the tomato sauce. Crumble or grate the cheese, then dot it all over the pizzas and bake as on page 127. You could add ham, salami or bacon, too, if you like.

Leftover chicken or meatballs Tear chicken into strips or crumble cold cooked meatballs (see pages 144–5) over the tomato base. Top with cheese and bake as on page 127.

Store-cupboard ingredients This is the time to get out all your bottles of Roasted Peppers and Tomatoes (see page 44), or olives, artichoke hearts and anchovies. Spread the dough with the tomato sauce, scatter over the toppings, then sprinkle with cheese. Pesto (see page 139) is gorgeous dolloped in small heaps over a tomato base between a pattern of roughly broken mozzarella, with torn basil or oregano on top.

Vegetables Think of spinach (with ricotta cheese and an egg) or steamed French beans (with prosciutto, jamon serrano or salami). Leftover roast vegetables really come into their own here – such as sweet potato, goat's cheese and thyme, or rounds of roast aubergine and garlic with a few dried chilli flakes. Put the vegetables on the tomato-topped pizza bases and bake as on page 127.

Pissaladière A French version of pizza, using one large piece of dough pulled out into a rough oblong that will fit an oiled metal baking tray or the underneath of a metal roasting dish. Spread the dough with 4 large onions that have been finely sliced and cooked in butter or oil until completely soft (or use Onion Marmalade, see page 42). Dot stoned black olives over the top and thin fillets of anchovies (in a criss-cross pattern is traditional), then bake as on page 127.

Tomato and anchovy A variation on pissaladière using Quick Tomato Sauce (see page 36) instead of onions, and with anchovy fillets as a topping. Tear basil leaves over and drizzle the whole lot with olive oil before baking.

Completely plain pizza bases These are good served with soup or dips. Prick the bases all over with a fork, drizzle with a little olive oil and strew crunchy sea salt and some dried or fresh thyme over the surfaces before baking.

Baguette Pizza

My mother made 'pizzas' out of baguettes right through the 1970s and I can't lose my taste for them. If you don't have time to make dough, they're the ideal solution.

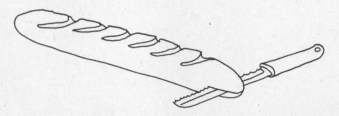

Simply cut a baguette into lengths, halve it as if you were making a sandwich and squish each half flat with the palm of your hand. You could take out some of the bread, leaving only a crusty shell, but this is not entirely necessary because the bread mops up the tomato sauce beautifully. Put the bread on a baking sheet, cover with tomato sauce and toppings of your choice, then bake at about 180°C/Gas Mark 4 for 7–10 minutes.

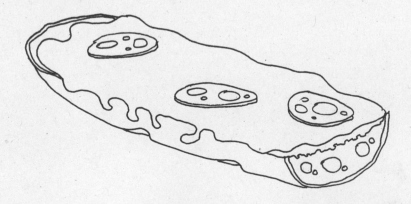

Fruit Pies

Just like meat and vegetables, fruit can be made into pasties, pies and wonderful tarts. Crisp flaky pastry is a great foil for soft fruit. I almost always use puff pastry, but you could choose shortcrust (see pages 110–11) instead.

A Simple One-crust Apple Pie

Unlike savoury pies, the filling doesn't have to be pre-cooked for a fruit pie. Just peel and core the fruit if necessary, dice it and put it in a pie dish – its juices will start to run as it bakes, and the steam created will help to raise the pastry into crisp flakes.

Serves 4

300g puff pastry
700–900g cooking apples, such as Bramleys
75g caster sugar
a little milk for brushing

Roll out the pastry on a lightly floured work surface to around 3–5mm thick. It should be large enough to cover a 1-litre pie dish with a good 2cm to spare around the edges. Leave it to rest for 10–15 minutes.

Preheat the oven to 200°C/Gas Mark 6. Peel and core the apples and cut them into medium-sized chunks. Put them into your pie dish, scatter over the caster sugar and add a tablespoon of water. Put a pie funnel in the middle of the dish.

To fix the pastry lid on to the pie, cut a thin ribbon of pastry, dampen the rim of the dish with a little water and press the ribbon firmly on to it. Brush the pastry ribbon with water, then lift the large sheet of pastry on to the pie dish and press the edges firmly on to the pastry ribbon underneath. Trim off any excess. Make a small slit with a sharp knife in the pastry over the pie funnel to allow the steam to escape. If you feel like it – and it takes seconds and looks marvellous – decorate the top of the pie by using leftover strips of pastry to make leaf shapes, sticking these to the top by brushing the underside with a little milk.

Brush the top of the pie with milk and place on a high shelf in the oven. Bake for 30–40 minutes, until the pastry is puffed and golden.

Also consider...

Some classic fruit combinations Replace a proportion of the apples with blackberries, rhubarb or raisins. According to what is in season, you can substitute damsons or gooseberries for the apples, or use apricots with toasted slivered almonds. Adjust the amount of sugar according to the kind of fruit you are using – if you prefer to be sure, you can part-cook the fruit in a large saucepan, adding the sugar to taste as the juices begin to run. In this case, let the fruit cool in the pie dish before adding the pastry top.

Puff pastry 'sandwiches' If you don't have very much fruit, individual pastry sandwiches make a really easy pudding that looks competent and takes only minutes. Roll out some puff pastry to around 3–5mm thick and cut it into oblongs about 10 x 5cm. Prick all over with a fork to prevent it puffing up too much. Place on a baking sheet and bake for 5–7 minutes at 200°C/Gas Mark 6, until risen and golden. Flip the pastry over, squash down with a spatula and bake for another 5 minutes. Sandwich 2 pieces of pastry together with a filling of fruit mixed with whipped double cream. Dust the whole lot with caster or icing sugar. Classic fillings include raspberries, strawberries, blackberries or stone fruits. Ripe pears are especially nice with a little diced stem ginger mixed into the cream with a teaspoon of its syrup.

No-dish fruit pie My mother makes fruit pies without using a dish by pulling up the edges of the shortcrust pastry into a rough, but still open, pasty that looks something like a pastry bowl filled with fruit and crusted with rough sugar. Roll out 300g shortcrust pastry (see pages 110–11 for home-made) or puff pastry into a rough oval, about 3–5mm thick. Slip it on to a greased baking sheet and leave in the fridge to rest for 20 minutes. Brush the pastry with beaten egg yolk and scatter over a handful of semolina to absorb some of the juices from the fruit. Pile about 700g prepared fruit into the middle of the pastry and pull up the edges like a rough basket around it. Brush the pastry with egg white and sprinkle with coarse sugar. Delia Smith made this beautiful pie famous using gooseberries.

Tarte Tatin Traditionally made with apples, but you can use pears just as well. I make the tart in a 20–22cm ovenproof frying pan. Use 400g puff pastry, 10–12 small, sharp dessert apples or pears (peeled, cored and sliced), 85g caster sugar and 55g butter. Very gently melt the sugar in the frying pan so that it turns into a caramel, making absolutely sure that it does not burn. Dot the caramel with the butter and then layer the fruit neatly in the pan, packing it in tightly and filling up any holes and spaces with bits of cut fruit. Cover with a circle of pastry rolled out to about 5mm thick, tucking the edges into the pan. Bake at 200°C/Gas Mark 6 for 20 minutes, until the pastry is puffed up and golden. Leave to cool for 10 minutes, then put a plate over the top of the pan and invert the whole lot so that the tart slips out on to the plate. Spoon off any excess juice and serve at room temperature.

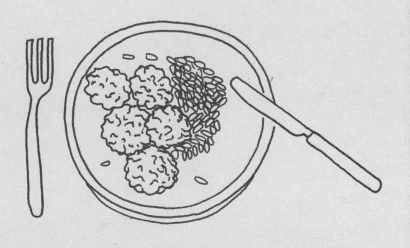

Potato Cakes, Rice Cakes, Fishcakes and Meatballs

Meatballs, fishcakes and so on are all, as our grandmothers well knew, a godsend for using up the ends of things. You don't need a huge amount of leftovers, and they also freeze very successfully, providing some of the best leftover-leftovers.

Unless you are up for careful, fine chopping, a food processor or small electric chopper will come in handy; use the pulse button to get a fine mince rather than a paste. Keeping your hands slightly wet when you're rolling or shaping the cakes helps prevent the mixture sticking – professional chefs get best results by rolling balls on the work surface rather than between their hands. Always chill them in the fridge for a good half hour before frying, as this helps them keep their shape in the pan.

This is when a box of breadcrumbs ready and waiting in the freezer is handy. Some recipes include them in the main mixture, while others use mashed potato, and you can also dip almost any ball or cake into a bowl of lightly beaten egg and then roll them in crumbs before you fry or bake them, which will give them a tantalisingly crunchy outside.

Potatoes

If you find yourself at a loss for things to do with leftover potatoes you can always add them to soups or stews (see pages 53–88).

Alternatively, here are two of my favourite ways to deal with them – one very simple and northern European, the other emphatically Italian. Both are wonderful for using up other leftovers or raw vegetables, and can be pepped up with either something from the store cupboard or a bunch of fresh herbs.

Potato Cakes

Use mashed potato for these or grated leftover boiled waxy potatoes (grating won't work with floury potatoes, as they will disintegrate). As with Bubble and Squeak (see page 151), you could mix equal quantities of potato with another vegetable – anything from cooked chopped spinach to grated leftover parsnips and just about everything in between.

It would be crazy to give a full recipe for potato cakes, since you simply need to make a mixture that will hold together well enough for frying in small patties. Use an egg for binding, adding it gradually so that you don't end up with a sloppy mix, any chopped herbs you like – dill, parsley and thyme are all lovely – and some seasoning. Shape into rough balls, flattening them down into 'burger' shapes. Shallow-fry until golden on both sides, or bake on a lightly oiled baking tray at 180°C/Gas Mark 4. Serve as a side dish with sausages, chops or stews, or on their own with a hearty chutney, Onion Marmalade (see page 42) or Chilli Jam (page 45).

You could also consider adding...

Onions or leeks Chop finely and soften in oil before adding potato.

Cheese Try a good handful of grated hard cheese or a little crumbled feta or goat's cheese.

Sweet potato cakes Add a few softened leeks and some fresh thyme to cooled sweet potato mash.

Spices Gently toast a teaspoon of ground spices, such as turmeric or coriander, in a dry frying pan for a minute or so, then add to the mashed potato. Alternatively, use a teaspoon of mustard or creamed horseradish.

Herby dumplings for beef broth or stew Use 55g mashed potato, 110g self-raising flour, a tablespoon of chopped parsley or thyme, salt and pepper. Mix all well, adding just a little water to bind, if necessary, and form into about 8 golf-ball-sized balls. Poach these in either broth (see pages 66–7) or a beef casserole. They will take only 5–7 minutes to cook.

Gnocchi

These little potato dumplings (*gnocchi* means 'lumps' in Italian) are a bit more fiddly to make than potato cakes but, like pasta, they are quick to cook and bland enough to absorb and carry any flavours you choose to add. They also give you a much-needed break from the ubiquitous spaghetti or penne.

My swelegant friends Emily and Ned profess never to cook with leftovers but they are past masters at gnocchi and this is an adaptation of their recipe. I regularly make too much mash on purpose because I love it so much. Though the mash has butter and milk added (which would normally make it too wet), it dries out considerably when it's been in the fridge for a day or two. Alternatively, use the oldest potatoes you can get your hands on – the longer they hang around, the more starchy they seem to get, and this is exactly what you need.

Whether you use leftovers or not, the mash for gnocchi must be really smooth. Push leftover mash through a sieve with the back of a spoon before using it; or for freshly boiled spuds use a potato ricer or mouli-légumes, or sieve them.

Serves 2

about 450g floury potatoes, peeled, boiled, drained thoroughly
    and mashed, or about 400g leftover mash
1 teaspoon salt
100–150g plain flour, plus extra for coating

1

Mix the cooled mashed potato with the salt and around half the flour to start with, using your hands to combine them and adding more flour as necessary, until you have a firm but slightly sticky dough.

2

Knead it briefly until smooth, using a little flour just to stop it sticking to your hands and the work surface, but not enough to make it crumbly.

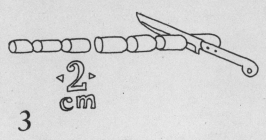

3

Roll the mixture into long sausage shapes, 1–2cm thick, then cut these into lengths of about 2cm.

4

You can now shape the little dough balls using 2 teaspoons to make rugby-ball shapes, or roll them between your palms to make spheres and then just slightly flatten them by squeezing gently with your finger and thumb.

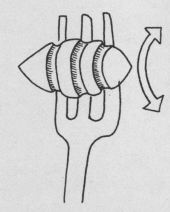

5

Roll each one lightly over the back of a fork to make grooves for the sauce to cling to. Put the gnocchi on a lightly floured tray and leave in the fridge until ready to cook. (In fact you can leave them overnight, or put them in the freezer for an hour if in more of a rush – chilling helps them to dry and firm up.)

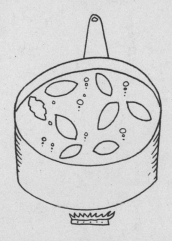

6

Cook the gnocchi in a large pan of salted simmering water for a minute or two – they are ready 10 seconds after they have floated to the surface. If you don't have a pan that gives them plenty of space, then cook in batches. Remove from the pan with a slotted spoon.

7

Serve simply with melted butter or a drizzle of good olive oil and a generous grating of fresh Parmesan, or with any of your favourite pasta sauces (see also the ideas overleaf).

Ideas for flavouring gnocchi and/or some simple sauces...

Ricotta cheese Replace the egg yolk with about a dessertspoon of ricotta cheese – just enough to make a fairly firm dough that is neither sloppy nor crumbly.

Chopped basil or any other herbs Add herbs to the mixture right at the start. In this case, serve with a home-made tomato sauce (see page 36).

Mushroom-stuffed gnocchi Make a ravioli-like parcel by rolling out the gnocchi dough thinly and cutting it into rounds about 6cm in diameter. To make the filling, sweat ½ finely chopped red onion with a crushed garlic clove. Add 140g of mixed mushrooms chopped very finely, a handful of finely chopped parsley, and some salt and pepper. Cook gently until the mushrooms are soft, then leave to cool. Top half the dough circles with a level teaspoon of the mushroom mixture and put another circle on top, pressing down around the edges to make a parcel. Cook in batches in a large pan of salted boiling water – once they begin to float, keep cooking for a further 2 minutes. Serve with grated Parmesan and a drizzle of olive oil.

Spinach-stuffed gnocchi Follow the method for mushroom-stuffed gnocchi, above, but for the filling, wash and chop a large handful of spinach and cook in plenty of rapidly boiling water for 3–4 minutes, until tender. Drain, cool and squeeze out excess water, then chop again very finely. Mix with a tablespoon of crumbled ricotta or goat's cheese and season well with salt and pepper.

Sweet potato gnocchi Substitute sweet potato for the ordinary potato and add some chopped thyme to the dough.

Pumpkin or parsnip gnocchi Replace some of the mashed potato with pumpkin or parsnips, either on their own or in combination. Peel and dice the vegetables and roast them in a dish in the oven at about 200°C/ Gas Mark 6 until tender but not crisp on the outside, then mash them. Let them cool before making up the gnocchi dough.

Sage sauce Melt a couple of tablespoons of butter in a pan (or heat some olive oil), add a good handful of chopped sage leaves and warm through. Pour the sage sauce over the cooked gnocchi and finish with grated Parmesan.

Puttanesca sauce Make the Quick Tomato Sauce on page 36, then add chopped anchovies, capers and chopped black olives to taste. Simmer until the sauce is very thick and has deepened in colour.

Pesto In a mini blender or food processor, make a paste from 2 peeled garlic cloves, ½ teacup of pine nuts, a teacup of freshly grated Parmesan and a large bunch of basil, adding olive oil until the mixture achieves the consistency of wet sand. Season to taste. Swirl a couple of teaspoons of pesto per person into the cooked gnocchi. Instead of basil and pine nuts, you could use walnuts with parsley, or substitute sun-dried tomatoes (or Bottled Dried Tomatoes, see page 44) for the basil.

Frozen peas and prawns Half a teacupful of each, cooked together swiftly in a little olive oil, makes a fantastic topping for cooked gnocchi. Scatter chopped mint, basil or parsley on top.

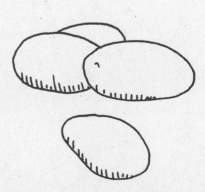

Arancini (Risotto Balls)

Arancini means 'little orange' and these re-fried risotto balls are such a staple of Italian leftover cooking that many families cook too much risotto on purpose so that they know *exactly* what they are having for lunch the next day. To my non-purist mind, risotto tastes better the next day anyway, and these impeccably simple balls have the added delight of a slight crunch on the outside. You can use any leftover risotto (see pages 176–7), including whatever ingredients you have added to flavour it.

Serves 2

2 teacups leftover risotto
1 egg, lightly beaten
about ½ teacup polenta (or plain flour and breadcrumbs instead)
olive oil for shallow-frying

Shape the leftover risotto into golf-ball-sized balls. Dip the balls in beaten egg and then roll them in polenta (or dust them with flour, dip them in beaten egg and then roll them in breadcrumbs). Chill for 20 minutes or so.

Heat 1cm of olive oil in a frying pan, add the risotto balls and fry gently until golden all over. If you like, you can push down slightly on the balls with a spatula to flatten them and turn them into crispy rice patties. Serve with salad or tomato sauce (see page 36).

Think about ...

Adding cheese It is traditional with arancini – especially if your leftover rice is plain – to push a small piece of cheese into the centre of the balls as you make them. Almost any cheese will do – mozzarella or Taleggio will both melt sumptuously, but goat's cheese or a cube of Parmesan are fine. I'm told red Leicester does the trick too. Make sure the cheese is completely enclosed by the rice.

Adding simple flavours to leftover plain risotto Parmesan, lemon zest and a little chopped tarragon; small pieces of tomato (or sun-dried tomato) and finely chopped basil; finely chopped strong mushrooms such as porcini or morels, fried in a little oil or butter until tender; diced roast pumpkin and goat's cheese; leftover fish or prawns, finely chopped, with lime or lemon zest. Add any of these combinations to plain leftover risotto rice before forming into balls, dipping in egg and frying.

Making suppli A traditional Italian way of using up Bolognese sauce and long grain rice or risotto rice. There are many regional variations in Italy, which allows us to use whatever we have to hand and think of it as classic. Mix the sauce and cooked rice together until firm enough to roll into balls of whatever size you prefer. Roll these in plain flour, dip them quickly into beaten egg and then roll in breadcrumbs. Traditionally, they are deep-fried, but I shallow-fry them in vegetable oil until golden on all sides. Delicious hot (with roast vegetables, say) and really useful cold in lunchboxes and for picnics.

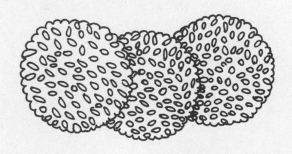

Fishcakes

The great thing about fishcakes is that they are *supposed* to be made with cold cooked fish so this is one recipe that doesn't turn how do to things 'properly' on its head. If you have leftover mash, so much the better. If using fresh fish, you will need to poach it first – in a frying pan is easiest – with milk just to cover, a knob of butter, a couple of peppercorns and a bay leaf. Bring to a gentle simmer, cook for 2–3 minutes, till the fish flakes when prodded with a knife, then leave to cool. Remove the skin, break the flesh into flakes and check for bones.

I use tomato ketchup in fishcakes. This sounds a bit odd, I know, but it adds a lovely sweetness while binding the cakes together. You can leave it out if you like, and add a little beaten egg instead for binding. You could also add a drop or two of anchovy essence if you have it.

Serves 2

160g cooked fish (ideally white fish or salmon), flaked
160g mashed potato
1 tablespoon tomato ketchup
1 teaspoon English mustard
a little plain flour
oil for frying
salt and pepper

Put half the fish in a bowl with the potato, ketchup, mustard and some seasoning and mix until smooth. Gently fold in the rest of the fish. Mould the mixture into 2 round cakes , then chill for a good half hour.

Lightly dust the fishcakes with a little flour, shaking off any excess. Heat a tablespoon or so of oil in a frying pan and gently fry the cakes on both sides until crisp and turning golden.

Serve with rice or a fine pasta such as linguine, along with a salad or steamed greens, such as spinach, kale or broccoli. A home-made tomato sauce (see page 36) is lovely with fishcakes, as is bottled chilli dipping sauce or Chilli Jam (see page 45).

To ring the changes...

Add sorrel sauce If you can lay your hands on sorrel, it adds a welcoming astringent note. Follow the instructions for White Sauce on page 32 but replace the milk with fish stock and a glass of dry white wine. Finish it with a dollop of cream and chopped sorrel leaves.

Use cooked leftover rice Replace the mash with an equal quantity of leftover rice, and the ketchup with a little beaten egg. Dip the cakes in the egg and roll them in finely blitzed breadcrumbs (or cornmeal or polenta) before frying.

Add grated hard cheese A good handful of finely grated Parmesan or other hard cheese can be added to the mixture. Leave out the tomato ketchup and use beaten egg instead to bind.

Add fresh herbs Chopped chives, a little dill or even finely sliced spring onions will perk up the flavour and add shards of green to the fishcakes.

Make a spicier mix Leave out the ketchup and the mustard. Add ¼ teaspoon of dried chilli flakes, a handful of finely chopped fresh coriander, a small grating of fresh ginger and a teaspoon of Thai fish sauce. Roll the cakes in fine breadcrumbs before frying. Serve with Chilli Jam (see page 45), or diced cucumber with a dipping sauce of rice wine vinegar, caster sugar and a little fresh chilli.

Make fishcakes with bulgar (cracked) wheat Substitute 80g bulgar for the potato. Soak it in cold water for 15 minutes, then drain. Mix with the fish, a finely chopped small onion, some chopped fresh coriander or parsley and a squeeze of lemon. Shape into small balls or cakes and shallow-fry.

Cheat with tuna Drain and flake a small can of tuna and mix it with a roughly equal quantity of mashed potato. Add a spoonful of toasted pine nuts, plenty of fresh herbs, a pinch of ground cinnamon and a scant squeeze of lemon juice. Dust with flour and cook as opposite.

Classic Meatballs

I've been playing around with Marcella Hazan's classic Italian meatball recipe from *The Essentials of Classic Italian Cooking* (Macmillan, 1992) for over a decade. Everyone loves them.

Serves 4

3 tablespoons milk
1 slice of bread, crusts removed
*   (or 2 tablespoons breadcrumbs)*
½ onion or 1 small shallot, finely chopped
about 450g leftover cooked beef, lamb, chicken or pork,
*   fat and gristle removed, very finely chopped*
a handful of parsley, finely chopped
3 tablespoons freshly grated Parmesan cheese, plus extra to serve
1 egg
breadcrumbs for coating
olive oil for frying
1 quantity of Quick Tomato Sauce (see page 36)
salt and pepper

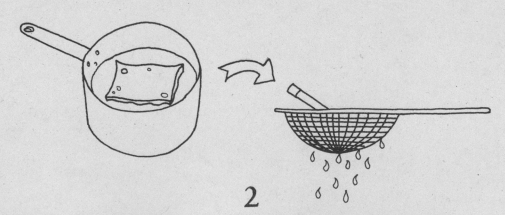

1
Warm the milk a little in a pan or the microwave.

2
Soak the bread in the milk, then strain it, squeezing out most of the liquid.

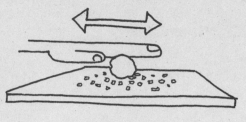

3

In a separate bowl, mix the onion, meat, parsley, Parmesan, egg, salt, pepper and the bready mush and combine well, using a fork or your hands.

4

Shape into balls about the size of a golf ball and roll them evenly in the breadcrumbs (no need for an egg dip here, as they should be moist enough already). Refrigerate for 30 minutes.

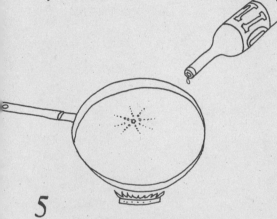

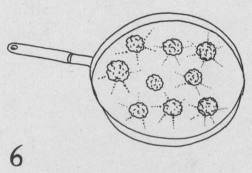

5

In a large frying pan or a wide saucepan, heat 5mm olive oil to shimmering point. The oil is hot enough when a breadcrumb dropped into it sizzles and floats on the surface rather than either sinking (not hot enough) or charring (too hot).

6

Add the meatballs in a single layer and fry gently until evenly golden and slightly crisp all over.

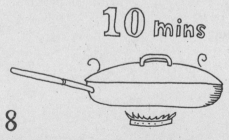

10 mins

7

Then just pour the tomato sauce over them.

8

Bring the sauce to a bare simmer and cover the pan (I use the top of my wok for this). Leave for about 10 minutes to heat the meatballs through in the sauce. Serve with rice, couscous, pasta or flatbreads, and with extra Parmesan grated on top.

Meatball inspiration ...

Mashed potato, lemon and garlic If you have a little mashed potato left over, use it instead of the milk-soaked bread and add a squeeze of lemon and some finely chopped garlic to the meat mixture. Shape into balls, roll in plain flour or breadcrumbs and cook as on page 145.

Turkey meatballs with sweet and sour sauce This has become an enduring post-Christmas supper in my house, inspired by a recipe in the book *Tony and Giorgio* by Tony Allan and Giorgio Locatelli (Fourth Estate, 2003). Follow the classic meatball recipe on the previous pages but use finely chopped cooked turkey and add a squeeze of lemon to the mix. Instead of the tomato sauce, fry 2 sliced onions very gently in 200ml olive oil with a bay leaf for 20 minutes or so, until meltingly tender. Soak 50g sultanas in warm water for 10 minutes, then drain and add to the onions with 100ml white wine vinegar. Simmer gently for 3 minutes and serve with the meatballs and rice or pasta.

Kofta, or kefta These Middle Eastern meatballs are traditionally made with raw meat but you can make your own approximation with leftover lamb, using an electric chopper to make a fine mince or, in this case, a paste if you prefer. Mix with finely chopped onion, flat-leaf parsley, soaked bread and egg, as on the previous pages, but add ½ teaspoon each of ground cinnamon and allspice to the mix and leave out the Parmesan. A little very finely chopped red pepper sweetens the mixture beautifully. Form into balls, omitting the breadcrumb coating, and cook as above. If you don't want to use tomato sauce, serve them as they are with a green salad, pitta bread and hummus, or yogurt and mint.

Turkish meatballs with spinach and chickpeas If you'd rather dispense with the tomato sauce, here's an alternative adapted from one of Claudia Roden's recipes. Make and fry the meatballs as on the previous pages. Wash and chop about 500g spinach and cook over a medium heat in a large pan of boiling water for 3–4 minutes, until just tender. Drain and squeeze out the excess liquid. Cook a finely chopped onion and garlic clove in butter until soft, then add the spinach with a drained 400g can of chickpeas and the meatballs. Add a little butter and enough stock barely to cover the meatballs, then cover and simmer for half an hour. Serve with plenty of chopped fresh coriander and some rice.

Beef balls with aubergine purée Another Turkish dish, which fares better with the stronger flavour of beef and uses up a single aubergine left in the fridge. Bake the aubergine in a hot oven (or grill it) until the skin blisters and the aubergine is soft. Peel off the skin, then mash the flesh in a bowl with a fork. Cook a finely chopped onion and garlic clove in a little oil until softened. Add the aubergine flesh, a squeeze of lemon and a tablespoon of tomato purée and season well. Cook for 7–10 minutes, then add the fried meatballs and simmer for 5 minutes, until the meatballs are warmed through. Lovely with toasted flatbreads.

Asian meatballs Leave out the tomato sauce entirely for this. Make the meatballs as in the main recipe, omitting the parsley and Parmesan and substituting ½ teaspoon of ground cumin, a good pinch of dried chilli flakes and some chopped fresh coriander. Shape into balls, shallow-fry in vegetable oil and finish with a squeeze of lemon juice. Serve with plain boiled rice.

Curry Add a tablespoon of chopped fresh coriander and ½ teaspoon each of ground coriander and cumin to the meatball mixture, omitting the Parmesan. Shape into balls and fry as in the main recipe. Then cook a finely chopped onion in oil in a frying pan with a finely chopped garlic clove, a 2.5cm piece of ginger, grated, and a finely chopped small green chilli. Add a 400g can of chopped tomatoes, a squeeze of tomato purée and a pinch each of ground coriander, ground turmeric, ground cinnamon and cayenne pepper. Simmer for 20 minutes, then add the meatballs, cover and simmer for 10–15 minutes. Add a little water or stock if the sauce is too thick.

Stuffed vegetables For a change, use the standard meatball mixture plus a bit of extra veggie flesh to stuff courgettes, aubergines or even tomatoes. For courgettes and aubergines, slice them in half lengthways and scoop out most of the flesh (with courgettes you will need to scoop out the seeds first). Chop the flesh finely and add to the meatball mix. If you prefer to use tomatoes, simply slice off the top, scoop out the flesh and add it to the mix with an extra tablespoon of breadcrumbs. Then just fill the vegetables up with the mix, drizzle with oil and bake for 10 minutes at 180°C/Gas Mark 4. Serve sprinkled with grated Parmesan.

Filo pastry Brush 2 sheets of filo pastry with a little oil or melted butter, place one on top of the other and cut out an oblong about 8 x 12cm. Fill with about a dessertspoon of the meat mixture. Fold the sides in over the meat and then roll up, like a cigar. Repeat with more filo until you have used up all the filling. Brush with beaten egg and bake on a lightly greased baking tray at 200°C/Gas Mark 6 for 10–15 minutes, until the pastry has puffed and crisped. These are particularly nice with Chilli Jam (see page 45).

Leftover-leftovers

- Meatballs in broth (see pages 66–7).
- Meatballs with pizza (see pages 126–8).
- Slice leftover meatballs into a pitta bread sandwich with a great dollop of mayonnaise or hummus.
- A couple of leftover meatballs can successfully be whizzed up into a soup for one, with the addition of a ladleful of good stock (see pages 28–9).

The Frying Pan
and the Wok

Frying pans or woks are brilliant for swiftly heating up leftover food. Think about leftover potatoes, fried with butter and garlic, or French beans tossed in hot oil with the last couple of rashers of bacon, and you get the idea. These are dishes that can be as simple or as complex as you like, using whatever needs to be cooked *tonight* with the added companionship of fresh herbs, a few spices or a bit of store-cupboard imagination.

This is not necessarily food that looks picture-perfect. But there's something about the idea of using only one big, broad pan that sits really happily with the whole business of leftover cooking – rustic, full of flavour and completely unassuming.

When it comes to the wok, I've described only two processes here – one for vegetables and one for meat. Once you've got these taped, you should feel confident on your own, even if, to start with, the very idea of a wok sends you cowering behind the kitchen table. You could stick to a large frying pan even for stir-fry recipes, though the good thing about woks – and you can get small, light ones that don't take up loads of cupboard room – is that they heat up food incredibly efficiently and fast.

Hashes

The French word *hacher* means to chop, or mince, and that says it all: hashes are unholy mixtures of meat and/or vegetables chopped and fried together in a wide pan. Brilliantly tasty, simple and cheap, and practically invented for leftovers and fridge clearouts.

Bubble and Squeak

This is one of the quintessential British leftover 'recipes'. It is a dish that can be made in tens of different ways according to what you have left over. At its heart are cabbage and potato, staples for British labourers since the seventeenth century. The exact proportion of potato to vegetable doesn't really matter.

It's very good as an accompaniment to sausages or bacon and egg. In fact, a fried or poached egg sitting astride freshly made bubble and squeak is Sunday brunch heaven. This recipe and all the variations that follow are perfect served with Tomato Chutney (page 43), Chilli Jam (page 45) or Onion Marmalade (page 42).

Serves 2

2 tablespoons oil, dripping or butter
1 onion, finely chopped
4–5 teacups mashed potatoes, or coarsely grated
or crumbled cold boiled potatoes
about 2 teacups cooked cabbage
salt and pepper

1

Heat half the oil or fat in a large frying pan, add the onion and cook gently until soft.

2

Mix the potatoes and cabbage together in a bowl, add the onion and season with salt and pepper.

3

Heat the remaining oil or fat in the frying pan, then add the potato mixture, pressing it down with the back of a wooden spoon to make an even patty that fills it to the edges. Cook over a moderate heat until golden underneath.

4

Break it up a little and turn over the lumps to brown the other side. Unlike a frittata or tortilla, bubble and squeak will not always hold together and, to my mind, is best served in a rough mountain of golden cabbagy crags. If yours does come out of the pan in one piece, you can cut it into wedges for serving.

Some more ideas...

To make individual patties Shape the mixture with your hands and, if you like a real crust, dust the patties with plain flour. You can either freeze these for later or shallow-fry them as on the previous page. Alternatively, brush them with melted butter or oil, place on a baking tray on the top shelf of an oven preheated to 220°C/Gas Mark 7 and cook for about 10 minutes on each side, until well browned.

Rösti Instead of using mashed potato and cabbage, grate cold boiled waxy potatoes (such as Charlottes or Jersey Royals) quite coarsely before cooking in one large or several small patties. You can mix carefully with other cooked vegetables, if you like. Use any combination of grated leftover root vegetables, including turnip, celeriac, swede, carrots and sweet potato.

Brussels sprouts, broccoli or kale These can all be used in place of the cabbage.

Potato and celeriac mash Mixing cooked mashed celeriac in with the potato mash adds a whole new dimension. Play around – you've nothing to lose by using spring onions instead of ordinary ones, or adding a teacup of grated carrot or a teaspoon of grainy mustard to the mix before frying.

Sweet potatoes Substitute these for ordinary potatoes; they're great with an equal quantity of cooked chopped leeks mixed in. Crumble in a little soft goat's cheese and chopped thyme, if you have them.

Cheese and herbs This is entirely a matter of taste. A handful of any crumbled or grated hard cheese will work very well added to the potato and cabbage mix with some finely chopped thyme or parsley.

Parsnip and apple A really amazing combination that rather turns bubble and squeak on its head. I make small patties from raw ingredients, using a large grated parsnip and a couple of grated dessert apples, bound with a medium egg. Add some torn pancetta or browned bacon, if you like. Dust with plain flour and shallow-fry in hot oil or butter. Really good served alongside sausages.

Trinxat This is the Spanish way with bubble and squeak, using potatoes, turnips, chicory, spring greens, garlic, thyme and bacon, all in a delicious combination. Roughly mash the cooked potatoes and turnips. Steam or boil chopped chicory and/or spring greens until tender and allow to cool. Mix the two together with a little chopped garlic and thyme. Fry some chopped bacon or pancetta until crisp and keep it to one side. Then fry the potato mix in the bacon fat until heated through and browning in places. Serve with the bacon pieces on top.

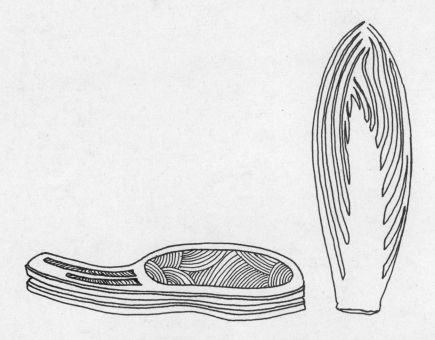

Swedish Pytt-i-panna
and Other Meat Hashes

Pytt-i-panna is a hash of particularly Scandinavian bent that you can adapt for almost any leftover meat, using chopped boiled potatoes or mash and an egg or not, as you like. This recipe comes from my Swedish friend, Christine, but, again, the amounts are only indications – just work with what you have available.

Serves 2

1 tablespoon oil, lard or butter
1 onion, chopped
4–5 teacups cold boiled potatoes, cut into cubes
2–3 teacups (about 300g) diced leftover meat (ham, bacon and
    sausage are traditional)
½ teacup breadcrumbs, lightly browned in a dry frying pan (optional)
salt and pepper

Heat the oil or fat in a large frying pan, add the onion and potatoes and cook until beginning to brown. Go gently – you don't want the potatoes to break up. Add the chopped meat and cook until thoroughly heated through. Season to taste. If you feel the need for some crunch, scatter toasted breadcrumbs on top.

Serve piled on to a plate, topped with a fried egg, if you like, and some pickled beetroot if you happen to have any.

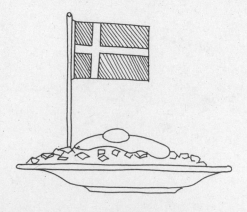

Some other meaty hash ideas ...

Hash browns Use boiled or roast potatoes and mash them roughly in a bowl. Add a sprinkling of raw spring onion (or an ordinary onion that has been fried until soft and brown), any chopped herbs you fancy, and some fried pancetta, bacon or lardons. Add a beaten egg to the mix if you like, then shallow-fry as one big cake or individual patties until golden brown. Sprinkle some herbs on top and serve with Chilli Jam (see page 45) or Onion Marmalade (page 42) for a perfect lunchtime snack.

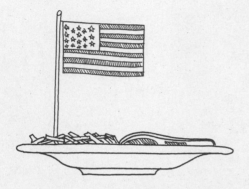

Lamb with parsnips or sweet potato Tear or dice the meat before adding to cooked diced or mashed vegetables. Add a pinch of ground cumin to the mix before frying.

Beef with swede and kale Tear or dice the meat and add it to mashed swede and finely shredded cooked kale before frying.

Pork with celeriac and leeks Tear or dice the meat and add it to mashed celeriac and finely sliced raw leeks before frying.

Christmas leftover hash Anything goes. Tear or dice any combination of leftover turkey, ham, bacon and sausages. Mash or dice any combination of leftover roast potatoes, parsnips and carrots. Finely shred leftover Brussels sprouts and crumble any leftover stuffings. Mix everything together, add a beaten egg or not, as you like, and shallow-fry in one big or several small patties. Finish with a handful of chopped herbs.

Rustic Fried Green Vegetables

There is no recipe as such for this dish because, frankly, the quantities don't matter and the vegetables you use will be determined by what you have available. It's a classic Mediterranean peasant dish made in the heaviest, widest frying pan you have – gutsy with garlic and fragrant with dry-earth herbs such as thyme, rosemary and sage.

I make this dish most when there are gluts of slim French beans around in mid-summer, so fresh that they hardly even need to be topped and tailed. If you want to speed things up, you could boil them for a scant couple of minutes first and drain them well. Almost any leftover green vegetables can be fried with potatoes like this, with a couple of cloves of garlic and some herbs. For spinach, broccoli and cauliflower, add a good pinch of dried chilli flakes too.

> *olive oil*
> *garlic – as many cloves as you like, roughly chopped*
> *slim French beans*
> *an equal quantity of leftover cooked potatoes, roughly diced*
> *thyme, rosemary or sage, chopped*
> *salt and pepper*

Heat some oil in a wide, heavy frying pan. Throw in the garlic first, followed by the beans and potatoes. Fry gently until the beans are cooked and the potatoes just turning golden, but watch that the garlic doesn't catch and burn or it will become bitter. Add some chopped herbs, stir well and cook for a couple of minutes, then season to taste.

Serve hot or, even better on a hot day, at room temperature, with a hunk of good bread.

Also consider...

Broad beans and fresh coriander If you grow your own broad beans, or know someone who does, gather up a few of them when they are very young and fry them in their pods with a good handful of coriander. Anything other than immature pods will be tough.

Middle Eastern spices You can use any green vegetables in this way. Keep the garlic but replace the herbs with chopped fresh coriander and add ground cinnamon and cayenne pepper to taste.

Mangetout A sweetly delicious alternative to beans. No need to blanch them first.

Fennel, potatoes and bacon Cook finely sliced fennel and chopped bacon along with the diced potatoes. Allow them all to brown gently in the pan.

Leftover meat Chicken, ham and pork work particularly well with fresh green vegetables. After Christmas, shredded chard is delicious with leftover diced ham.

Cured meat The last few slices of chorizo, salami or prosciutto can all be added to the pan – particularly good with French beans or mangetout.

Black pudding and parsnips Any kind of leftover sausage is lovely with diced parsnips. Use leftover parsnips, or fry diced raw parsnips (in place of the potatoes) and let them soften before adding the sausage.

Two Frying Pan 'Stews'

The frying pan is really useful for making quick 'stews' of leftover meat, cut into strips and coated with a rich creamy or herby sauce. In some ways, the process is very similar to making the pie fillings on pages 115–19, though because pastry is not involved, the stews will be sloppier.

The two recipes that follow specify beef and chicken, but no one's holding you to it – and each can be easily adapted for the kind of leftovers that you want to use up.

Beef 'Stroganoff'

Of *course* stroganoff is best when made with strips of raw beef fillet. But the memorable thing about it is its strong mushroom and cream sauce and the classic recipe can be adapted for using up the remains of the beef joint. Happily, beef leftovers are generally pretty rare, which helps to keep them juicy as well as deepening the flavour of the dish.

Serves 4

a little butter or oil
1 onion, finely sliced
2 tablespoons plain flour
2 tablespoons paprika, plus extra to serve
4 teacups (about 400g) leftover beef, cut into strips
300g small mushrooms, wiped and sliced
a small glass of white wine
200ml beef stock
250ml soured cream
a small bunch of parsley, chopped
salt and pepper

Heat a little butter or oil in a wide frying pan, add the onion and cook until just turning golden.

In a bowl, mix the flour and paprika with a good pinch of salt and a grind of pepper. Toss in the beef strips, making sure that they are well coated. Shake off excess flour and then add the meat to the onion, turning it in the oil until they are well amalgamated. Add the mushrooms and stir well for a minute. Add the wine, stir again and simmer for 2 minutes. Pour in the stock, bring to the boil and simmer gently for 5–10 minutes, until the mushrooms are tender. The dish should not be sloppy – the point of the flour is to thicken the sauce. Add the cream and heat through very gently for a couple of minutes – don't let the mixture boil or the cream will separate.

Serve hot on a bed of rice or flat noodles, sprinkled with a little paprika and the chopped parsley.

Change things about...

Chicken or pork Simply replace the beef with strips of these meats instead. If using pork, then consider substituting strong wild mushrooms for the cultivated ones. Or you could reconstitute some dried mushrooms in a bowl of warm water according to the instructions on the packet – squeeze them well before adding to the dish. Finish with a squeeze of lemon and some finely chopped dill.

Spinach and lamb Leave out the mushrooms. Wash a large bunch of spinach and cook quickly in just the water clinging to its leaves, until wilted. Squeeze out excess liquid and chop roughly. Add to the stroganoff right at the end, with a grating of nutmeg.

Tomatoes My mother made a version of this dish by cutting out the flour and paprika and replacing the stock and cream with a can of chopped tomatoes and a teaspoon of tomato purée, which made it not a stroganoff at all, but tasty all the same. Add the tomatoes and tomato purée to the cooked onion and simmer for 7–10 minutes, until reduced and thickened. Then add strips of beef and heat through thoroughly. Serve with chopped parsley.

Chicken Fricassée

Fricassée is the name given to a mixture of meat or vegetables fried in a light sauce. This recipe pairs chicken with its closest friends, garlic, lemon, rosemary and wine. It's quick and summery and is at its best served with a half-and-half mix of basmati and wild rice, plus a green salad. If there is anything left, consider using it as a pie filling (see pages 115–19).

Serves 2

1 tablespoon olive oil
2 teacups (about 200g) cooked chicken, torn into pieces about 4 x 2cm
1 large garlic clove, finely chopped
a sprig of rosemary or a good pinch of dried rosemary
3 tablespoons dry white wine
juice of ½ lemon
zest of ½ lemon, taken off in long strips with a zester

Heat the oil in a frying pan, add the chicken and cook over a medium heat for a minute to warm through without browning too much. Add the garlic and rosemary and cook, stirring, until the garlic is tender but not browned. Add the wine and leave it to bubble for half a minute, so that the alcohol evaporates, then turn down the heat and simmer slowly for 5–10 minutes, until the liquid has reduced slightly.

Transfer the chicken to a serving plate with all its juices. Return the pan to the heat and add the lemon juice and zest. Simmer gently for a minute before pouring the whole lot over the chicken.

Ring the changes by adding...

Crunchy vegetables Raw green beans or finely sliced fennel would be nice added to the pan and cooked until tender before the chicken goes in. If you have leftover vegetables, add them after the wine.

Mushrooms Add a heaped teaspoon of chopped thyme to the chicken at the start. Finely slice a handful of mushrooms and add them at the same time as the chicken pieces.

Red cabbage Add finely sliced red cabbage to the pan right after the chicken and substitute red for white wine.

Stir-Fries

I love the noise of liquids sizzling as they hit the hot wok and the sound of the metal spatula scraping against the sides. Both simply shout that supper's nearly ready (and that there won't be much washing up). Whatever ingredients you are using, if you can pick up a pack of bean sprouts or a can of water chestnuts on the way home, both will add the nutty crunch that makes these dishes irresistible.

Bottled Chinese sauces such as black bean, yellow bean or oyster will all add extra flavour. You'll need to check the instructions on the bottle, as each brand or type needs more or less cooking and they vary in strength. As a rule of thumb, when stir-frying for 2 people you should use 2–4 teaspoons of sauce: too much will be overwhelming, so err on the side of caution to begin with.

There is a handful of things to bear in mind when stir-frying:

- First: have all the ingredients prepared upfront. Once you start cooking, the point is speed.
- Second: heat the wok before adding the oil. This prevents food sticking.
- Third: make sure the oil is shimmering hot (but not smoking) before adding the ingredients, or they will become oily and limp.
- Fourth: be quick and definite about adding ingredients and tossing them briskly in the hot oil with a metal spatula or a wooden spoon.
- Lastly: if you are using raw rather than leftover vegetables, the order in which you add them is important. Tougher ones should be cooked first and the most tender ones last. Spinach and Chinese leaves have a high water content and can make the other vegetables soggy, so add them right at the very end; they need only a minute.

Basic Vegetable Stir-Fry

Leftover vegetables are not ideal for wokking but this is the perfect time to use up an array of fresh vegetables that are on the turn, cooking them in strict order so that tougher vegetables such as carrots come well before softer ones such as mushrooms or peas. Keep things straightforward by flavouring the oil simply with garlic, chillies or ginger, or experiment with bottled Chinese sauces. Serve vegetable stir-fries as a TV supper, with rice, noodles or just on their own.

Serves 2

1 tablespoon vegetable or groundnut oil
1 onion or a bunch of spring onions, finely sliced
1cm piece of fresh ginger, finely chopped or grated
1 garlic clove, crushed
3–4 teacups mixed vegetables, cut into fine florets or dice – broccoli,
    cauliflower, carrot, pepper, French beans, fennel, cabbage, courgette,
    asparagus tips and mangetout are all great, depending on the time of
    year and availability
a handful of bean sprouts, if you have them
3 tablespoons soy sauce

To serve:
sesame seeds, toasted in a small frying pan
    without oil until just browning
    (watch them, as they burn easily)
sesame oil

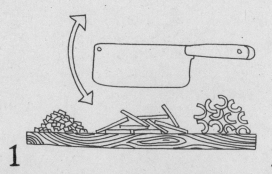

1 First prepare and chop all your ingredients.

2 Heat a wok over a fairly high heat, then add the oil and heat until shimmering.

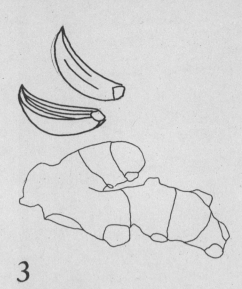

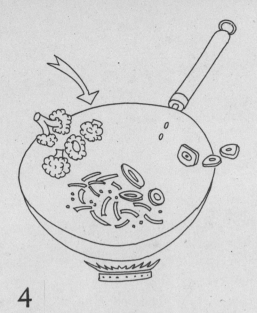

3

Add the onion and stir for a minute, then add the ginger and garlic and stir well for about 30 seconds.

4

Add the thickest or hardest vegetables first (carrots, cauliflower, broccoli and the like) …

BEAN SPROUTS
GO LAST

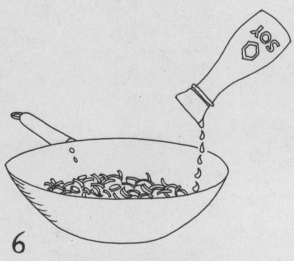

5

… with softer vegetables such as courgette following as each becomes tender (but not soft – you want to keep a bit of crunch here). Bean sprouts, if you are using them, will take only 30 seconds to cook, so add them right at the very end.

6

Finally, add the soy sauce, toss well and serve immediately, with a scattering of toasted sesame seeds and a drop or two of sesame oil.

A Leftover Meat Stir-Fry

In a classic meat stir-fry, the meat is marinated in oil and flavourings, then flash-fried right at the start. Then you remove it from the pan while the vegetables and sauce cook, returning it to the wok right at the end.

If you are using leftover sliced chicken, pork, beef or lamb, you have to invert the cooking process, adding it at the end and giving it just enough time to heat really thoroughly – a minute or so – or it will become dry and tough. As with vegetable stir-fries, use simple garlic, chilli and ginger flavour combinations or experiment with bottled Chinese sauces.

This recipe describes the basic process for a leftover meat stir-fry but you can refine and alter it endlessly, depending on your own taste. In general, try to choose the rarest pieces of meat and slice them into strips around 3 x 1cm.

Serves 2

1 tablespoon sesame or vegetable oil
1 garlic clove, finely chopped
2.5cm piece of fresh ginger, grated
a handful of mangetout (optional)
1 tablespoon soy sauce
2–4 teaspoons oyster sauce
    (check the instructions on the bottle,
        as strengths differ)
1–2 handfuls of bean sprouts (optional)
a small bunch of pak choi (or any Chinese greens),
    roughly shredded
1–2 teacups (about 200g) leftover meat, sliced into
    smallish pieces
sesame seeds, toasted in a small frying pan without
    oil until just browning, to serve

Heat a wok over a fairly high heat, then add the oil and heat until shimmering. Add the garlic and ginger and stir well. If you have mangetout, throw them in now, and keep turning the whole lot around in the hot oil for a minute or so. Add the soy sauce and oyster sauce and cook for another 2–3 minutes. Add the bean sprouts, if using, and the pak choi or Chinese greens, and stir briskly for a scant minute, until the greens have wilted. Finally, add the meat, moving the whole lot around for a minute until thoroughly heated through.

Serve sprinkled with toasted sesame seeds and accompanied by rice or noodles.

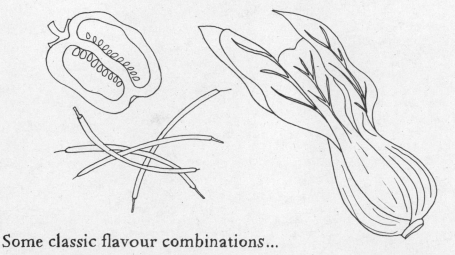

Some classic flavour combinations...

Beef and black bean sauce Fry chunks of white onion and green pepper in oil until just becoming tender (the peppers should still have a little bite left at the end, so don't overcook them). Add the black bean sauce and cook according to the instructions on the bottle, then add strips of beef just to warm through.

Leftover meat and coconut Flash-fry some chopped red chillies and a piece of bruised chopped lemongrass. Add a couple of lime leaves, a tablespoon of Thai fish sauce, a teacup of coconut cream and a teaspoon of brown sugar and cook for 2 minutes. Add the meat and heat through, then serve with rice and with basil scattered on top.

Pork and yellow bean sauce Start with onions and carrots, cut into fine strips, followed, if you like, by strips of red or yellow pepper. Add the sauce according to the instructions on the bottle, then toss in the meat and heat through. Add a handful of cashew nuts right at the end for crunch.

More leftover meat stir-fries...

Lamb and chilli Follow the main recipe but omit the oyster sauce and, if you like, replace the mangetout with green beans. Fry ½ deseeded and finely chopped red chilli with the garlic and ginger, and add an eggcup of sherry at the same time as the soy sauce.

Pork or chicken with basil and pepper Flash-fry finely chopped garlic, a rounded teaspoon of ground black pepper and ½ chopped red chilli for a minute. Add 2 lime leaves, some torn basil and 2 tablespoons of soy sauce and cook for 3 minutes. Add the meat and heat through. Asparagus tips are good with this, too – add them at the same time as the soy sauce.

Rice

I know the general rule for uncooked rice is to use about 80g per adult but I still nearly always cook too much of it and I'm pretty sure I'm not alone. Despite the fact that its price has rocketed recently and its scarcity has brought down governments, the latest statistics suggest that we throw away around 85,000 tonnes of it a year in the UK. Like pasta, it provides an almost instant meal in itself but – unlike pasta – it's endlessly versatile: there are even dishes that *have* to be cooked with cold leftover rice (fried rice is a case in point). The recipes that follow don't use only leftover rice, though: there are also several quick and tasty ways of using both short and long grain rice cooked from scratch as vehicles for the usual array of leftovers or tired vegetables.

I have to warn you to be careful with rice. *Bacillus cereus* is a very common cause of food poisoning, and one of its favourite haunts is cooked rice left in a warm place, or even at room temperature, for several hours. The spores are heat resistant and brief reheating such as stir-frying doesn't break down their toxins, so it's not entirely surprising that the bacteria is commonly associated with Chinese restaurants and particularly with re-cooked rice. This kind of food poisoning is usually relatively mild – but who needs it? The best precaution is not to leave leftover rice (or, in fact, potatoes or pasta either) lying around. Put it into an airtight box once tepid and refrigerate immediately.

Perfect Plain Rice

To start at the very beginning, great fluffy rice is not hard to achieve even without an electric rice cooker. The problem with drowning the rice in a great pot of water and then straining it is that it will never achieve that soft dryness that sucks up sauces so well. For that, you need to use the 'absorption method', which is much more straightforward than it sounds.

My friend Vineeta's method goes like this:

1 measure of long grain rice
2 measures of cold water
a small knob of butter (to prevent the
*   rice sticking to the bottom of the pan)*

1

Put the rice, water and a very small knob of butter into a pan with a tightly fitting lid.

2

Bring to a bare simmer, put on the lid (you could also wrap a tea towel round the lid of the pan before putting the lid on to get a tight fit) and cook for 10 minutes, then turn off the heat. Do not remove the lid for 10 more minutes.

3

The rice will need to be fluffed gently with a fork before serving.

To flavour rice

Include a cardamom pod, a lemon wedge, a cinnamon stick, a bay leaf, a couple of cloves, 1cm of peeled fresh ginger or a star anise in the pot. The flavour will not be intense but the scent will be seductive. Remember to remove the spices before serving.

Three Ways to Rescue Leftover Rice

You can reheat rice really simply by plunging it into rapidly boiling water for 30 seconds before draining it well and serving. But I think this is the moment to add a few extra flavours and ingredients, to turn it into something better than its plain self.

Simple Spiced Rice

Nothing could be simpler than adding some sweetly browned onion and gentle spices – in fact, there is some evidence that adding turmeric to reheated rice not only tinges it with its marvellous colour and flavour but inhibits bacteriological activity as well. You could use leftover boiled potatoes instead of rice in this dish.

Serves 2

1 tablespoon olive oil
1 onion, thinly sliced
1 garlic clove, finely chopped
1 teaspoon ground cumin
1 cinnamon stick or ½ teaspoon ground cinnamon
2 cloves
2 cardamom pods, lightly crushed
1 bay leaf or 3 curry leaves
2–3 teacups cooked long grain rice, preferably basmati
finely chopped fresh coriander, to serve

Heat the olive oil in a pan, add the onion, then cover and cook gently until soft. Remove the lid, add the garlic, spices and bay leaf or curry leaves and cook gently until the onion just begins to turn brown – it will add a caramel depth to the rice when they are mixed together.

To refresh the cooked rice, tip it into rapidly boiling water, bring the water back to the boil for 30 seconds, then drain very thoroughly. Fork the onion mixture into the rice with all its oil. Scatter chopped fresh coriander on top, then serve warm with pitta bread and plain yogurt or Ash's Spicy Carrot Pickle (see page 47).

You could also consider...

Lentils *Kichri,* as this dish is known in India, is an ancient staple food (and the origin of Anglo-Indian kedgeree). Substitute cooked lentils or split peas (either leftover or from a can, warmed through first) for half the rice.

Toasted nuts or dried fruit Scatter a good handful of toasted pistachios or flaked almonds over the spiced rice right at the end or, alternatively, a handful of raisins.

Spicing things up Add ½ deseeded and chopped red chilli to the onion as it cooks.

'Tempered oil' Instead of adding browned onion to the rice, flavour it simply with oil and spices. Heat a couple of tablespoons of oil in a small pan until shimmering but not smoking. Add your favourite flavour: some lemon zest, chopped ginger, garlic or fresh chilli, or a couple of cardamom pods, a star anise, some cumin seeds or a cinnamon stick. Keep the heat on moderate and stir the flavours around, removing them with a slotted spoon before they colour or burn. Fork this flavoured oil through the refreshed rice and then scatter chopped coriander on top.

Kedgeree Flake almost any leftover cooked fish into the gently spiced rice, just enough to warm it through. Smoked haddock is traditional, but ends of smoked salmon are also good. You could even use a small can of tuna. I like to add a knob of butter and a dollop of single cream to make the dish richer and moister. Scatter a few chopped spring onions or parsley over the top before serving.

Pilaf

Adding leftover rice to the frying pan turns it, in effect, into a pilaf.
A true pilaf (or pilau, if you prefer) should of course be made with raw
rice simmered in oniony, spicy stock and you *can* do it this way, adding
leftover meat or vegetables right at the end once the rice is cooked. But
you can also make a pretty good approximation with a spare bowl of
rice that will take half the time.

The bonus is that this is also a great way of clearing the fridge of
needy vegetables or leftover meat.

Serves 3

1 onion, finely chopped
1 large garlic clove, crushed
a little butter or olive oil
1 teacup leftover or raw vegetables, cut into small pieces
1 teacup leftover meat, shredded fairly small
1½–2 teacups (160–200g) leftover rice
salt and pepper

To serve:
a handful of parsley or other herbs, finely chopped
plain yogurt

Gently cook the onion and garlic in a little butter or olive oil in a frying
pan, letting the onion brown to add sweetness to the dish. Add the
vegetables. Leftover vegetables will simply need to heat through, but if
they are raw, cook until they are tender. Add the meat and rice and
season well with salt and a little pepper. Move the mixture about until it
is hot right through. Serve in a bowl, with a handful of chopped parsley
or your favourite herb and a dollop of tart plain yogurt.

Some more ideas...

Leftover chicken Use a teacup of leftover chicken with mangetout,
French beans, peas or broad beans, adding a handful of basil and a
squeeze of lemon juice before serving.

A Moroccan twist Add spices to the cooked onion, heating them for 3–5 minutes before adding the rice. I use a teaspoon of ground cumin, a good pinch of ground cinnamon, ½ teaspoon of ground coriander or a cardamom pod. Before adding the rice, add a good handful of raisins or currants and a few strands of saffron steeped in an eggcup of hot water. When everything is heated right through, squeeze a little lemon juice over the dish and serve with torn parsley or coriander leaves and toasted flaked almonds, and/or some almost-crunchy browned sliced onion.

Moroccan leftover lamb or chicken The leftover meat can be added either on its own or with the Moroccan spices listed above. Serve with a bowl of natural yogurt mixed with chopped mint.

Fennel, sultanas and pine nuts Add very finely sliced fennel to the onion and garlic. Brown rice (or even bulgar wheat) is especially good with this combination, with the addition of a tablespoon of sultanas and another of toasted pine nuts. (To toast pine nuts, just put them without oil into a small, heavy-based pan and place over a medium heat, stirring pretty constantly until turning golden. Don't take your eye off them for a moment, as they burn easily.) Once the rice is warmed through, fork in a good handful of chopped fresh coriander or the chopped fronds of the fennel. Serve hot or at room temperature.

Red cabbage and sultanas Finely shred some cabbage and add it to the onion and garlic at the start. When the cabbage is tender, add a tablespoon or two of sultanas and then the rice, heating it through thoroughly. The cabbage will stain the rice carmine, but it's worth it for the taste.

A paella-style dish Use a mixture of pork, chicken and shellfish in whatever quantities you have around. The whole thing, inauthentic as it is, can be gilded by infusing a few strands of good saffron in an eggcup of hot water for 10 minutes and pouring the liquid into the pan before adding the rice and meat.

Leftover fish Melt a tablespoon of butter in a frying pan, flake some leftover fish into it, along with the leftover rice, and heat through, stirring gently as you go. Grated lemon zest, some torn basil leaves and lots of freshly ground pepper would be lovely here. Because both leftover fish and rice can be dry, add a heaped teaspoon of butter at the end.

Oven pilaf This calls for uncooked rice and leftover meat. Sweat the onion and garlic in an ovenproof casserole, add joints of leftover poultry or sausages (or both), add 1 teacup of basmati rice and 2 teacups of stock or water, then cover tightly and bake at 180°C/Gas Mark 4 for 15–20 minutes, until the rice is tender, light and fluffy. Season to taste and serve with plenty of fresh herbs forked in, and Ash's Spicy Carrot Pickle (see page 47).

Fried Rice

Fresh rice is no good for this dish – it is designed for leftovers. If you don't have a wok, use a frying pan, as hot as you can get it. In either case, make sure the oil is shimmering but not smoking before you begin cooking. Have all your ingredients ready before you start – you really can add any vegetables or leftover meat that you want to use up.

Serves 2

2 tablespoons vegetable or groundnut oil
1 small onion or 3 spring onions, chopped
1 egg, lightly whisked
about 2 teacups (200g) cold cooked rice, straight from the fridge
1 tablespoon soy sauce

Heat the oil in a wok or frying pan, add the onion and fry, stirring well, for 2 minutes, until softened. Turn the heat to moderate, add the egg and stir briskly for a minute to make scrambled egg. Add the rice and soy sauce and stir for 2–3 minutes, turning the mixture constantly, until everything is very well heated through.

You could add ...

Leftover meat Shredded chicken is ideal, or even the last rasher of bacon snipped into pieces and browned with the onion. Add cooked meat just before the rice goes in.

Frozen prawns I leave out the egg for this. First fry the onion as opposite, with a finely chopped garlic clove. Add the rice and fry for a couple of minutes. Add a handful of defrosted cooked prawns and cook for 2 minutes. Stir in the soy. Garnish with a few finely chopped spring onions.

Vegetables Defrosted frozen peas, a red pepper cut into small dice, small broccoli or cauliflower florets, even carrots – anything goes when adding vegetables to this dish. If they are already cooked, add them with the rice to heat through. If raw, add them to the onion, the thickest or toughest ones first, adding each subsequent vegetable as the one before it has become tender. Remove the vegetables from the pan and cook the egg as opposite. Return the vegetables to the pan with the rice and toss well.

Risotto
and its American Cousin

Both risotto and jambalaya are heart-warming dishes that use raw rice, cooked from scratch, and both are ideal for using up leftovers. But in other ways they are only distant cousins. First, risotto uses short grain Italian rice, such as Arborio, Carnaroli or Vialone Nano, which swells and goes creamy as it cooks, while jambalaya uses long grain rice, which has a dryer, fluffier texture. Second, risotto calls for one or two simple flavours only, while jambalaya – as its name suggests – is something of a fridge-clearer: with this dish, it's a case of the more the merrier. Don't be put off by the myth that risotto is difficult; it's just that it demands attention, asking to be stirred pretty constantly over the 20 minutes that it takes to cook. Jambalaya, on the other hand, is not so needy.

A Plain Risotto

There is much debate about the ideal texture of risotto – sloppy and almost soup-like on the one hand, firmer and dryer on the other. It's a taste thing. I prefer to err on the side of wetter rather than dryer and I have no problem with the comforting idea of eating risotto with a spoon. In the end, it's entirely up to you.

Once you've made a plain risotto, the variations are infinite. Just remember to add leftover meat, fish or vegetables at the last minute, giving them time to warm through properly without falling apart or losing their bite. Because they will not add much flavour to the rice as they cook, add stronger tastes at the end of the process as well as at the beginning: finely chopped garlic or aromatics such as celery and fennel are good at the start, and the freshest herbs you can get your hands on at the end. Use the best Parmesan you can find (but don't include it with fish).

I make risotto just as often with leftovers as I do with fresh ingredients. Nor do I mind reheating it for lunch the next day. I also go out of my way to cook too much risotto every time, because there's a delightful Italian thing to do with the leftovers – Arancini (Risotto Balls), see pages 140–1.

Serves 2

about 500ml vegetable (or chicken) stock – home-made (see pages 27–30)
    or made with vegetable bouillon powder
1 tablespoon olive oil
1 small onion or shallot, very finely sliced
200g risotto rice
2 tablespoons vermouth or dry white wine (optional)
a knob of butter
a good handful of freshly grated
    Parmesan cheese, plus extra to serve
salt and pepper

1
Heat the stock in a pan and keep it at a bare simmer.

2
In a separate pan, heat the olive oil, add the onion or shallot, then cover and cook gently until softened.

3

Add the rice and stir it well, so that each grain is coated in oil.

4

Add the vermouth or wine if using (or a ladleful of stock) and let it bubble, stirring well, for 30 seconds or so, until it has been absorbed by the rice. The rice should begin to look creamy.

5

Keeping the pan over a low heat, add a ladleful of stock and stir pretty constantly to encourage that creaminess to develop.

6

As the rice absorbs the stock, add another ladleful and repeat the process until, after 15–20 minutes, the rice is cooked but not falling apart: it should have a very slightly nutty bite to it. The stock should be just about used up, but it is impossible to be absolutely precise about how much you will need. You may have a little stock left over, or you may have to top it up with some hot water from the kettle.

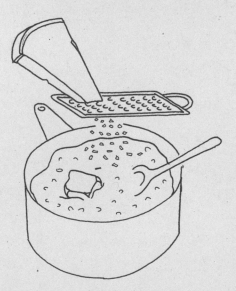

7

Once the rice is cooked, gently stir in the butter and Parmesan and season to taste. Serve immediately, with more Parmesan at the table to grate over the top, accompanied by a crunchy green salad.

Risotto in every colour of the rainbow...

Leftover chicken and lemon Add 1–2 teacups of meat and the zest of ½ lemon about 5 minutes before the rice is cooked. A few frozen peas would be nice here too. To ring the changes, roast sweet potato or lightly browned sliced fennel could be added with the chicken.

Frozen peas Defrost about 1½ teacups of peas. Cook half of them gently in a good tablespoon of butter. Add a tablespoon of grated Parmesan when they are tender and whiz into a green gloop in a food processor. Stir this through the cooked rice, along with the whole peas. It will turn a luscious spring green. Scatter chopped mint or basil, and more Parmesan, on top.

Broad beans or asparagus Add 1–2 teacups of broad beans or asparagus, chopped into 2–3cm lengths, to the rice, giving them just enough time to cook (about 6–8 minutes). Scatter over torn prosciutto right at the end.

Frozen prawns 1–2 teacups of defrosted cooked prawns (or cooked fish, broken into pieces) can be added once the rice is cooked, along with plenty of chopped herbs such as parsley, basil or sage. Use fish stock if you have it. You could substitute fennel or leek for onion at the start. Omit the Parmesan.

Leftover beef Cut the rarest pieces into strips, adding them with some very finely chopped rosemary and sage once the rice is cooked. Use a glass of red wine rather than white wine at the very start.

Mushrooms Fry 1–2 teacups of sliced mushrooms in a little olive oil or butter until tender. Beef up the flavour, if you like, by adding some reconstituted dried mushrooms, following the instructions on the packet and squeezing them well before chopping them and cooking with the rest of the mushrooms. Keep all these to one side. Add a crushed garlic clove to the onion at the start. Make the risotto as usual and add the mushrooms once the rice is cooked, giving them just enough time to heat through. Finish with the Parmesan and a good handful of chopped parsley.

Roasted peppers or sun-dried tomatoes Use bought or home-made (see page 44). Both are delicious on their own or with leftover chicken and lots of herbs. Add them 5 minutes before the rice is cooked.

Onion Double the quantity of onion, using whatever variety you have, slicing them finely and softening them in oil right at the start. If you like, replace the vermouth or white wine with a glass of sweet sherry or Marsala and add a sprig of rosemary to the rice as it cooks (and remove it before serving). Separately fry a few more onions until golden and use as a final flourish over the top, along with some more grated Parmesan.

Beetroot Use leftover roast beetroot, or roast it first in the oven at 180°C/Gas Mark 4, then slip off the skin when cool. Chop roughly. Add to the risotto 5 minutes before the rice is cooked. It will, of course, turn the rice pale purple as it stains each creamy grain.

Parsnip Peel the parsnips and dice them quite small, then add to the onion at the start, softening them for 5–10 minutes. If you have it, replace the white wine with cider. When the risotto is ready add lots of cheese – Parmesan or a creamy, mild, blue cheese such as dolcelatte (so Richard, my editor, tells me – this is his recipe).

Jambalaya

This spicy rice dish from the southern states of America uses long grain rice and just about anything you have lying around. It's a great vehicle for mixed vegetables, with either leftover chicken or frozen prawns. Don't be alarmed by the length of the ingredients list below – just use what you have and ignore whatever you don't.

This recipe is just a starting point. For example, to make use of Christmas leftovers, use ham and turkey together, adding a 400g can of chopped tomatoes after the onion has cooked and reduce the quantity of stock accordingly. You could also convert it into a pasta dish by replacing the rice with small pasta such as macaroni, which gives the Creole thing an ironic Italian twist.

Serves 4

2 tablespoons olive oil
1 onion, finely chopped
2 garlic cloves, finely chopped
2 hot chillies, deseeded and finely chopped, or 1 teaspoon chilli flakes
3 or 4 sausages or 1 good-sized chorizo sausage, skinned and chopped
360g long grain rice
1 bay leaf
1 tablespoon ground turmeric
½ teaspoon paprika
1.3 litres stock
any mixed vegetables you have: a couple of red peppers, cut into
*   strips, for example, and a teacup or two of diced courgettes, peas,*
*   beans or cauliflower florets*
2 teacups (about 200g) diced cooked chicken
2 teacups (about 200g) defrosted raw prawns
salt and pepper
Tabasco sauce, to serve (optional)

Heat the oil in a large, heavy-based pan, add the onion, garlic and chillies and cook until softened but not browned. Add the sausages or chorizo and cook until the fat begins to run and they start to colour. Add the rice, bay leaf and spices and stir well so that the rice is coated in the oil and flavourings. Add the stock and bring to a simmer. After about 10 minutes, when the rice is half cooked, add the vegetables and then the leftover chicken and continue to simmer until the rice is just about done. Watch the rice: if it is just covered by stock, all will be well, but if it begins to look too dry, add a little more stock as needed.

Stir in the prawns and mix well. Turn off the heat, put the lid on the pan and leave for 3–4 minutes, to allow the prawns to cook in the heat of the rice. If you are using tiger prawns, however, you will need to add them with the chicken, as they will take 10 minutes to cook; smaller prawns will need almost no cooking and will become tough if overdone. Season to taste and serve hot, with a dash of Tabasco sauce for more bite.

Pasta

Pasta is best freshly cooked in loads of bubbling salted water. About 100g is enough for an adult but it's one of those things that I (and almost everyone else I know) regularly cook too much of, and there is not a great deal you can do with the leftovers. Actually, I don't mind yesterday's pasta and sauce warmed up in the microwave for lunch the next day – I find the ease and the stodge of it rather comforting. The few simple ideas in this chapter work well and they are delicious enough to make you think twice about sending cold pasta to landfill.

Refreshed Pasta,
with Several Quick Sauces

To refresh un-sauced leftover pasta, just plunge it into boiling water for 20 seconds, then drain and serve. Yes, it will be 20 seconds overdone but you don't live in a restaurant. Alternatively, stir the pasta into a heated sauce. With a good fresh sauce, some flavoured oil or a swirl of home-made pesto (see page 139), you'd be hard pressed to tell the difference.

Quick sauces for refreshed pasta...

Aglio e olio The simplest pasta sauce of all is good olive oil in which finely chopped garlic has been gently heated (but don't let it colour or it will become bitter). You could also add a good pinch of dried chilli flakes. Once the oil is warm and the garlic tender, spoon the whole lot through refreshed pasta and serve with some finely chopped parsley.

Rustica Heat a great glug of good olive oil with some chopped walnuts, anchovies and garlic, then spoon the mixture through the refreshed pasta. Scatter lots of fresh basil and grated Parmesan over the top.

182

Anchovy Heat good olive oil with a nice fat anchovy fillet or two per person. Fork the flavoured oil through the refreshed pasta and throw over a little parsley and grated Parmesan to serve.

Broccoli and anchovy Cut some broccoli into small florets and toss them with chopped anchovies in olive oil over a medium heat until tender. Then just fork through refreshed pasta.

Baby spinach and ricotta cheese Soften chopped garlic in olive oil, add some big handfuls of baby spinach and turn in the oil until wilted. Spoon this through refreshed pasta and crumble some soft ricotta on top.

Onion marmalade Add a heaped spoonful of Onion Marmalade (see page 42) to refreshed pasta with some toasted chopped walnuts. Crumble some blue cheese over the pasta to serve.

Tomato sauce Heat some home-made tomato sauce (see page 36) and add leftover pasta to it, leaving it to warm through for 30–60 seconds.

Pesto A gorgeously gutsy sauce of basil, pine nuts and grated Parmesan – see page 139. Simply toss with refreshed pasta.

Petits pois and lemon zest Warm some lemon zest in olive oil, then stir through the refreshed pasta with some cooked petits pois.

Red onion and fromage frais or mascarpone Cook a finely sliced red onion in a little olive oil until soft. Add fromage frais or mascarpone and warm through. Add leftover pasta to the hot sauce and let it heat through for 30–60 seconds.

Sausage or cured meat Use leftover cooked sausages with a pinch of dried chilli flakes, or the ends of salami, chorizo or other cured meat. Cook a finely chopped small onion in olive oil until soft, then add the meat and warm through for a scant minute. Spoon the mixture through refreshed pasta and scatter over parsley and Bottled Dried Tomatoes or Roasted Peppers (see page 44).

Baked Pasta,
Several Ways

This simple bake has strong tastes to perk up day-old pasta and is so good that I sometimes cook too much pasta on purpose so that I can eat it the next day. It is best made with pasta robust enough to hold its shape on second cooking, such as penne or fusilli. This recipe, and most of the variations below, uses unsauced pasta, though almost any leftover sauced pasta can be reheated in the same way, with a good covering of cheese or a tomato sauce and a topping of cheese.

Serves 2

about 200g leftover penne or fusilli
a jar of pesto or 1 quantity of home-made pesto (see page 139)
1 quantity of Quick Tomato Sauce (see page 36)
250g mascarpone cheese
freshly grated Cheddar or Parmesan cheese

Preheat the oven to 180°C/Gas Mark 4. Put the cold, cooked pasta into a buttered ovenproof dish. Swirl in the pesto, then cover with the tomato sauce. Add a layer of mascarpone and finish off the whole lot with a good grating of Cheddar or Parmesan. Bake for about half an hour, until the mixture is bubbling and the cheese is browning.

You could also consider...

Replacing the sauces listed above with one of the following combinations. Consider, too, using almost any of the ingredient combinations for bakes (see pages 98–100 and 102–3).

Ratatouille Mix the ratatouille on pages 80–1 with leftover pasta (and the mascarpone, if you like) and bake as above, with a good grating of cheese over the top.

Leftover chicken and mushroom Gently fry a couple of teacupfuls of sliced mushrooms with a clove or two of garlic until softened. Add the pasta and a teacup of leftover chicken torn into shreds, then swirl in some mascarpone. Top with either grated cheese or Flavoured Breadcrumbs (see page 49) before baking.

Canned tuna Drain the fish, mix with a tub of mascarpone and add the leftover pasta. Top with grated Parmesan and bake as opposite.

Macaroni cheese Make the Cheese Sauce on page 32, stir in the pasta and top with grated cheese before baking. For extra flavour and colour, you could add some baby leaf spinach or some broccoli, cut into florets small enough to cook through in the baking time.

Pastitsio This is a traditional Greek way of baking pasta with a moussaka-like nutmeggy white sauce. Add a good grating of fresh nutmeg to White Sauce (see page 32), then remove from the heat and beat in an egg or two. Scatter some breadcrumbs over the base of an ovenproof dish, then add grated cheese, cooked macaroni and Bolognese sauce (or ragù, see pages 78–9). Finish with the eggy sauce and top with more grated cheese. Bake as opposite.

Mozzarella and diced ham A great way of using up a Christmas ham. Dice the meat, mix with a little mascarpone and the pasta, then top with some slices of mozzarella and bake.

Leftover chicken or bacon Add torn leftover chicken or cooked bacon to the basic recipe.

Aubergines Stuffed with Pasta

This is not only a great dish to make with leftover pasta but a lovely thing to do with aubergines too, and it makes a filling and pleasingly Mediterranean supper with hardly any fuss.

Serves 2

2 aubergines
200g leftover pasta
½ quantity of Quick Tomato Sauce (see page 36)
1 tablespoon chopped basil
1 tablespoon chopped parsley
1 ball of mozzarella cheese, diced
olive oil for drizzling
½ teacup freshly grated
*   Parmesan cheese*
salt and pepper

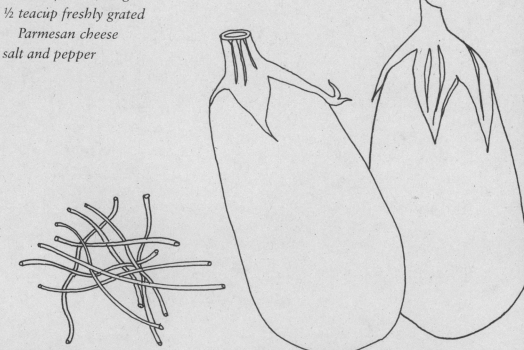

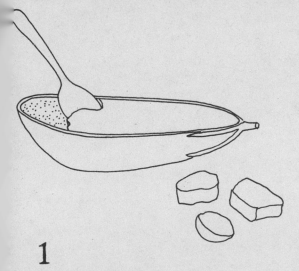

1

Preheat the oven to 200°C/Gas Mark 6. Slice the aubergines lengthways in half and scoop out most of the flesh with a metal spoon.

2

Chop the aubergine flesh finely, mix with the pasta, tomato sauce, herbs and mozzarella and season to taste.

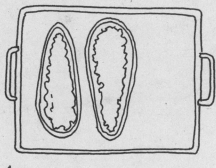

3

Stuff this mixture into the aubergine shells, drizzle some olive oil over them, then scatter over the grated Parmesan.

4

Place in a roasting tin and bake for 15 minutes, until the aubergine skin is wrinkled and the filling heated right through.

You could also consider...

Stuffed courgettes Choose large courgettes or small marrows instead of aubergines. Halve them lengthways, scoop out the seeds and discard. Then scoop out the rest of the flesh and proceed as above.

Italian Fried Pasta

Pino, the owner of our favourite family Italian restaurant, tells me that it is not unusual at all for Italians to mix leftover pasta – complete with its coating of sauce and Parmesan – with eggs, frying the whole lot into a thick omelette. It sounds better in Italian: *frittata di pasta*.

The dish is designed for sauced pasta. If you want to make it with plain leftover pasta, then first add a little sauce or flavouring from the ideas for refreshed pasta on pages 182–3. It is important not to use pasta covered with a great river of sauce, however – if necessary, drain off some of the liquid before using it. Quantities are not really an issue, since it's a dish that you throw together with whatever you have lying around. It won't suffer if the ratio of pasta to egg is slightly different from the one I've suggested below.

As a general rule of thumb, use 2 eggs for each 100g leftover pasta. Beat the eggs lightly in a bowl and add ½–1 teacup of grated Parmesan and the leftover pasta with its scant coating of sauce. Heat a little oil in a deep frying pan and add the egg and pasta mixture. Turn down the heat and cook for 2–3 minutes (or longer if you are using more than 2 eggs), until the omelette is sealed underneath and almost set on top. Put a plate over the pan and turn out the omelette on to it, then slide it back into the pan, cooked-side up, and cook until firm underneath (instead of turning the omelette, you could just put the pan under a medium grill until the top is lightly golden). Serve warm with a green salad.

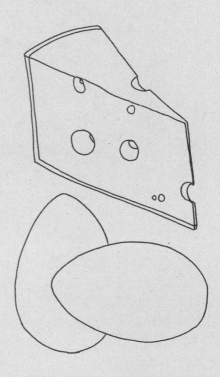

Eggs and Cheese

We Brits used to have a passion for using up leftovers at breakfast, often simply mixed with an egg. But we've lost the time (and the knack) for making cooked breakfasts, so most of these recipes are for lunches and suppers instead. Omelettes are simple and fast, while pancakes still have something of the excitement of Pancake Day about them, and soufflés – which don't need to be complicated at all – somehow make everyone feel special.

Cheese is a perfect partner for many of the egg recipes that follow, so they make good use of the bits left in the end of the packet. It's worth storing the ends of hard cheese in an airtight box, or grated in a sealed container, for just these eventualities, never mind for Toasted Cheese (see pages 201–2). In the fridge, these ends will keep for several weeks, by which time you'll probably have used them all up.

Making simple cheeses when you have too much milk hanging around is not only easy but incredibly satisfying. Home-made cottage cheese actually tastes of something, and paneer, a denser, sliceable cheese, is just plain hard to get in most shops.

Omelettes for All Occasions

It is almost absurd to suggest what you might include in an omelette because, really, anything goes. Asian cooks take it for granted that yesterday's leftovers can be bound with a fluffy egg to make a kind of deconstructed breakfast pancake.

Cheese Omelette

There have been centuries of debate about how to cook the perfect omelette. For me, it boils down to keeping it small and cooking it fast: the general rule is about 45 seconds to 1 minute per egg. French omelettes should never be flipped like pancakes to cook on the second side. Instead they are folded into thirds; they will then finish cooking in their own heat in the time it takes to get them to the table.

Serves 1

2 eggs
a handful of grated hard cheese
a drop of milk (optional)
butter for frying
salt and pepper
chopped herbs, to serve (optional)

Break the eggs into a bowl, add the cheese, the milk if using, and some salt and pepper and mix very roughly with a fork.

Heat a small, heavy frying pan. Add a large knob of butter and wait for it to foam, but not brown. Pour in the mixture and for the first 10 seconds move it around with a wooden spoon or a spatula, as you would for scrambled eggs, until the eggs just begin to set. Then let it cook over a medium heat without stirring, gently pulling the sides away from the edge of the pan into the centre to let any liquid egg run from the centre to the empty edge.

After a minute or two, it should be cooked but still slightly shiny and runny on top. Fold one edge into the middle and then fold the opposite edge on top of that – in effect folding the whole thing into thirds. Slide on to a plate, scatter over herbs, if you like, and eat immediately.

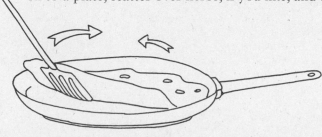

More omelette-y ideas...

Meat or fish leftovers Finely shredded or diced cooked meat or fish, or crumbled bacon, can be added to the omelette mixture once you've stopped stirring and the eggs are cooking. Scatter chopped herbs over the omelette to serve.

Leftover vegetables Dice leftover cooked vegetables finely and add to the mix at the start. The rule here is that there are no rules. Grated ends of cheese are good with the vegetables.

Canned tuna This is lovely crumbled into the eggs once they are cooking, with a little very finely chopped shallot or onion and chopped parsley. Omit the cheese.

Store-cupboard ingredients A few capers, a chopped anchovy fillet, sliced artichoke hearts, or Bottled Roasted Peppers or Dried Tomatoes (see page 44) are all delicious in a simple omelette, added once the eggs are beginning to cook.

Leftover potatoes Make a faux tortilla by slicing and frying a few leftover potatoes first. Add a teaspoon of wholegrain mustard to the egg mixture and then drop the potatoes into the centre of the omelette just before it is cooked.

After Christmas Diced turkey is very good with a few rinsed capers and sliced or diced mozzarella. Add them all to the pan once the eggs are beginning to cook.

Scrambled eggs Scrambled eggs are also a great way of using up leftover chicken, fish or even vegetables. Cut them small and stir into scrambled eggs when they are just set.

Spanish/Italian Omelette

Both Spain and Italy have traditional omelettes – tortilla in Spain and frittata in Italy – made with lots of eggs and cooked into a more solid, sliceable dish than a French omelette, eaten either hot or at room temperature. Tortillas are denser, using sliced potatoes, but both are fantastic vehicles for an infinite array of leftovers and ideal for picnics.

I've conflated the two slightly different dishes here to describe a basic process. You can use whatever ingredients you have to hand. This is where the store cupboard comes in very handy indeed: Bottled Roasted Peppers or Dried Tomatoes (see page 44) will add sweetness, while artichoke hearts from a jar will give you something to bite on. I prefer the taste of red onions to white, but have stopped using them because they turn weirdly blue inside their eggy casing.

Serves 2

5 eggs
1–2 teacups (about 200g) meat or vegetable leftovers
    (see pages 194–5 for suggestions)
a good pinch of salt
1 tablespoon olive oil
1 small onion, sliced

Whisk the eggs in a bowl and add the leftovers and the salt. Leave to rest for 5 minutes.

Heat the oil in a medium, heavy-based frying pan, then add the onion and cook, stirring, until it is just starting to colour. Pour over the egg mixture and cook over a medium heat until the base of the omelette is set and beginning to brown and the top is just a little runny. Now you need to flip the omelette over. The easiest way is to put a plate over the frying pan and invert the whole lot until the omelette is on the plate, cooked-side up. Then slide it back into the pan (raw-side down) and cook for a further couple of minutes to set the egg. Alternatively, put the pan under the grill to brown the uncooked top lightly.

Once cooked, slide the omelette out on to a clean plate and serve hot or cold, cut into wedges.

Lots of ideas for ingredients...

Cold boiled potatoes Slice the potatoes and brown them gently in a little butter or oil in a frying pan. Add them to the eggs with some chopped herbs, if you have them, and a chopped garlic clove. Leftover kale or broccoli could also go in here.

Cold boiled potatoes and cheese Slice the potatoes and add them with some crumbled cheese while the omelette cooks. Blue cheese is particularly luscious but most other cheeses, especially goat's cheese, also taste great with potato. Add a few thyme leaves, too.

Ham, prosciutto or jamon serrano These are ideal with sliced leftover boiled potatoes, prepared as above. Simply shred the meat roughly before adding to the eggs or directly to the omelette as it cooks. You could also add cooked asparagus, cooked spinach or some thinly sliced cooked fennel. Grate some Parmesan into the omelette as it begins to set.

Bacon Lightly fry the last couple of rashers in the fridge and roughly chop them. Add them along with some chopped parsley, sliced spring onion and a grating of Cheddar, if you like.

Fish Any leftover fish works well, as does flaked canned tuna or defrosted cooked prawns. Include a tablespoon of chopped tomato and a handful of chopped parsley, or try something more Scandinavian with smoked salmon and chopped dill.

Chorizo and red onion Use a red onion and add some diced or sliced chorizo to the eggs, plus a little fresh thyme or oregano, if you have them.

Leftover chicken Tear it into strips and add to the egg mixture with a good teaspoon of Onion Marmalade (see page 42) for sweetness, and some thyme leaves.

Vegetables Any leftover vegetables can be used, including carrots, peas, beans and the like. Courgette and aubergine omelettes are particularly good for summery picnics – grill or brown the diced vegetables in a pan first and add to the eggs with some chopped spring onions.

Cheese and vegetable All the classic combinations work well here: broccoli or cauliflower with Cheddar; spinach and ricotta; leek and goat's cheese or feta; sweet potato and feta.

Italian fried pasta See page 188.

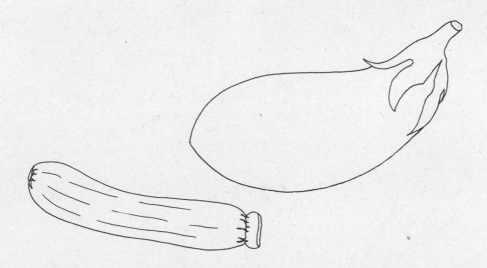

Savoury Pancakes

If you want to be grand about it, you could call these crêpes, and I'm not sure why they are so popular on the Continent and yet ignored here. As a dedicated pancake lover, I find this contrary.

Filled pancakes are brilliant for using up leftovers. I make the batter first and then let it stand while I get the fillings ready. You can do it the other way around – batter does not need to stand – but, whatever you do, have a bowl of filling ready before you embark on the frying bit. Instead of standing at the stove making a production line of individual pancakes, I prefer to preheat the oven and make them all in one go: filling, rolling, then lining them up like soldiers in an ovenproof dish. A quick grating of cheese and they can go straight into the oven until the cheese has melted; then everyone can eat at the same time.

Use the shallowest frying pan you have, ideally around 20cm in diameter, and the heavier the better. Get it really hot with a very little shimmering (but not smoking) vegetable oil. This is harder to achieve with butter because it burns easily and tastes dreadful when it does.

Makes 10–12 pancakes

110g plain flour
2 large eggs
270ml milk (or milk mixed with a
*   little water, if you prefer)*
2 tablespoons melted butter
a pinch of salt
your choice of filling (see page 198)
2–3 tablespoons vegetable oil
hard cheese, such as Cheddar or
*   Parmesan, for grating*

1

Put the flour, eggs, milk, butter and salt in a bowl and mix with a hand whisk or electric beater until you have a smooth batter with the consistency of thick pouring cream. Leave to stand while you prepare the filling – see the suggestions overleaf.

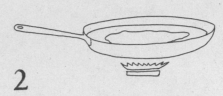

2

Preheat the oven to 180°C/Gas Mark 4. To make the pancakes, heat the oil in a 20cm frying pan. When it is shimmering hot, pour all of it out into a mug or bowl. This will leave just the right amount of hot oil coating your pan.

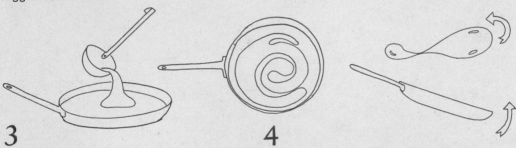

3

Use a ladle to pour a little pancake batter into the pan, then lift the pan off the heat, tilting and swirling it so that the batter runs fast right around the pan, completely coating the bottom in a thin layer.

4

Cook over a medium heat for 30–60 seconds, until golden and just crisping on the underside. Flip it over and cook the second side, then turn it out on to a plate.

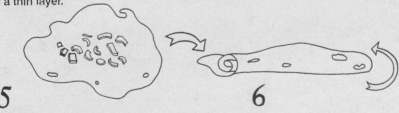

5

Fill with a couple of tablespoons of whatever cooked mixture you have ready, roll the pancake up and put it in an ovenproof dish.

6

Repeat with the remaining pancake batter and filling, re-oiling the pan when necessary.

7

When the dish is full, grate the cheese all over the pancakes and bake for 10–15 minutes, until the filling has heated through and the cheese has melted. Serve with a green salad.

Recommended savoury fillings...

Bear in mind that if the filling is too liquid, the pancakes will turn into soggy disasters, but if too dry they will be claggy. What you are aiming for is a mixture that holds its shape without being sloppy.

Chicken and/or ham Used chopped leftover chicken and/or ham with any combination of cooked bacon, mushrooms, peas, broad beans or sweetcorn in a creamy sauce (see Pies, pages 115–19). Scatter parsley, chives or tarragon over the pancakes, once cooked, and serve with Chilli Jam (see page 45).

Spinach with ricotta cheese Mix cooked chopped spinach with crumbled ricotta cheese, toasted pine nuts, chopped basil and perhaps some Bottled Dried Tomatoes (see page 44). You could serve these pancakes with Quick Tomato Sauce (see page 36).

Cheese Will generally perk up any cooked vegetables: think broccoli or leeks with a mustardy cheese sauce (see page 32), or soft goat's cheese with sweet potato or cauliflower.

Leftover fish or canned tuna Flake the fish and mix with some sweetcorn and Cheese Sauce (see page 32). Add a little chopped dill, if you have some.

Ratatouille See pages 80–1.

Recommended sweet fillings...

You could add a tablespoon of caster sugar to the batter if you really want to sweeten things up. Leave out the cheese from the recipe, of course, and serve immediately rather than baking in the oven.

Fruit Use up softening bananas by slicing them into pancakes with a squeeze of honey or a dribble of maple syrup. In fact, almost any ripening fruit can be used up in the same way (see pages 131–2 and 234–5).

Nutella spread Spread a thin layer over each pancake, roll up and serve.

Two Recipes Using Separated Eggs

The reality is that if you make a recipe using an egg white or yolk, you are going to be left with the other half of the egg. Yolks don't freeze well, though they will keep in the fridge in a covered bowl for up to 4 days. Whites can very happily be frozen in a strong bag. But the thing is, Hollandaise Sauce (see page 35), Mayonnaise (page 34), Custard (page 33) and Zabaglione (page 200) are brilliant ways of using up egg yolks, while whites can be added to omelettes (see pages 190–5), soufflés (see pages 203–5) or sorbets (see page 233). At the very least, there are two simple and heavenly puddings to be made entirely out of yolks or whites. Here they are.

Meringues (whites)

I rarely get round to freezing egg whites, since meringues are the easiest thing to make and keep for weeks in an airtight box or tin. Since electric whisks often end up beating all the air out of egg whites, I use a rotary whisk for this. Meringues are lovely sandwiched together with whipped cream or served with poached or baked fruit (see pages 238–40).

For each egg white, you will need 55g white caster sugar. Preheat the oven to 120°C/Gas Mark ½. Put the egg whites in a large bowl and whisk to firm peaks. Whisk half the sugar into the egg whites and then, using a large metal spoon, very gently fold in the second half of the sugar. Put spoonfuls of the mixture on to a baking sheet lined with baking parchment and bake for 1–2 hours, depending on size. The meringues should harden without colouring. Leave to cool completely on a wire rack before storing; alternatively, turn off the oven when the meringues are just about ready and leave them in the oven while it cools.

Zabaglione (yolks)

This classic Italian version of the old-fashioned British posset or American eggnog is sumptuously rich and sweet. I think it's perfect with just a few tart berries, such as redcurrants or early raspberries, if you can pick up a small punnet on the way home.

You don't need a double boiler to make zabaglione – a ceramic or glass bowl over a pan of gently simmering water will do. Just make sure the water is not even close to touching the bottom of the bowl or you will make sweet scrambled eggs.

Serves 2

2 egg yolks *(make sure there is no hint of egg white)*
2 tablespoons caster sugar
2 tablespoons Marsala *(or sweet sherry, if you have no Marsala)*

Whisk all the ingredients together in a bowl until really light and fluffy. Set the bowl over a pan of simmering water and whisk constantly (an electric whisk makes this easier) for about 5 minutes, until the mixture thickens and doubles in volume. Spoon or pour the shiny mixture into glasses and serve immediately.

Toasted Cheese

What could be simpler than cheese on toast – and what better way to use up all the ends of cheese in the fridge? Though soft goat's cheeses are lovely melted on to toast and served with salads or soups, for a filling dish on its own there's nothing better than toasted mature English cheese, such as Cheddar, red Leicester and so on – cheeses with a slightly sharp edge. Ideally, use a really thick slice of nutty brown bread for this.

Serves 1

a thick slice of bread
a teacup or so of grated or sliced ends of cheese
Worcestershire sauce (optional)

First toast one side of the bread under the grill. If you like Worcestershire sauce, mix up to a teaspoon (depending on your taste) into the grated cheese. Turn the bread over and squash the grated cheese over it in a layer about 1cm thick (or layer thin slices of cheese on it, if you prefer). Then simply grill the whole lot until the cheese is bubbling.

Some other ways with toasted cheese...

Welsh rabbit Gently melt 110g grated cheese, 30g butter and ½ wineglass of brown ale until bubbling, then pour it over toast. Try it. It's delicious.

Buck rabbit Welsh rabbit with a poached egg on top.

Leek rabbit Cook sliced leeks gently in a little oil until softened. Toast the bread on one side, spread the other side with a thin layer of Dijon mustard and put the leeks on top. Cover with a good strong Cheddar cheese and grill.

Cayenne Use a pinch of cayenne pepper instead of Worcestershire sauce.

More toasted cheese ideas…

Anchovy paste, mustard or Marmite These are lovely spread thinly under the cheese.

Croque Monsieur This can be an open or a closed sandwich, toasted, with a slice of good ham between the toast and the cheese.

Mushrooms on toast Lightly fry sliced mushrooms in butter with some finely chopped garlic and parsley, then spoon them over a thick piece of toast. Grate over a good layer of Parmesan and grill or bake for a couple of minutes until the cheese has melted. Though this is neither an egg nor a cheese dish, it is – at a long stretch of the imagination – a variation of cheese on toast, whipped up with just as little fuss.

Using up odds and ends of cheese My grandmother thought nothing of keeping bits of cheese without their rinds until she had enough to melt slowly in a pan with a teaspoon of English or French mustard. She poured the molten cheese into a small ramekin (or pot), allowed it to cool and then covered it with a thin layer of melted butter. This she kept in the fridge for sandwiches. It's actually a rather eighteenth-century idea, and a quick way to make toasted cheese.

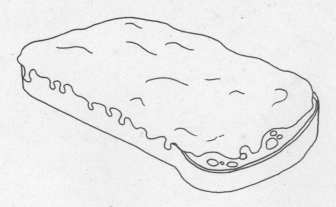

The Noble Soufflé

My mother taught me how to make a basic soufflé when I was about ten years old and it never fazed me – then. I suppose I'd never heard the general stuff about disasters, so I just went ahead and did it confidently and I can't remember it not working. As an adult, though, I carry all the normal baggage about soufflés: the fear of them not rising and the waste of food, time and effort if a runny sludge emerges from the oven rather than a gloriously adept puffball.

There is a science behind how eggs behave, so it's important to know the rules. But if you follow them carefully, soufflés become quick fallbacks for suppers or lunches – a brilliant means of using up the last of the cheese, or even a cup of green vegetables left over from dinner the night before.

At the heart of a good soufflé are a creamy white sauce enriched with egg yolks and a separate bowl of egg whites whisked into firm peaks. Electric whisks tend to fly away with you: it's harder to stop at the 'peak' stage and easy to beat all the air back out of the whites before you know it. Rotary whisks are much better for this.

You can make the yolky base a little in advance, but once you've whisked the whites, don't leave them standing around. When you come to folding the two together, it's a good idea to use a large metal spoon. First take a spoonful of the beaten egg white and stir it gently into the mixture to loosen it. Then fold in the rest of the whites gently but swiftly.

Once the soufflé is in the oven, leave it to do its thing uninterrupted: it's true that it gets a fright if you open your oven too early, and might collapse. Always serve it as soon as it's puffed up and ready.

The perfect partner for soufflé is a simple crispy green salad, just lightly dressed – there's something intrinsically 'right' about this combination of colours, textures and tastes.

A Cheese Soufflé

The simplest of all soufflés and a brilliant way of using up the ends of hard cheese like Cheddar or Parmesan.

Serves 2–3

25g butter
25g plain flour
150ml milk
75g strong hard cheese, finely grated
3 large eggs, separated
salt and pepper

Preheat the oven to 200°C/Gas Mark 6. Butter a 900ml soufflé dish (about 20cm in diameter).

Now make a white sauce: melt the butter in a small pan, add the flour and stir well over a low heat for a minute. Gradually add the milk, whisking as you go to prevent any lumps forming. Bring to a bare simmer and allow the sauce to thicken for 2–3 minutes. Remove from the heat, stir in the cheese, then season and pour into a good-sized bowl (to give you space to add the egg whites later). Leave to cool for 5 minutes or so, then stir in the egg yolks.

In a separate bowl, whisk the egg whites until they form firm peaks. Gently stir a spoonful of the whisked whites into the cheese sauce to loosen it and then softly fold in the rest. Pour the mixture cleanly into the soufflé dish and put on to the centre shelf of the oven. Bake – without opening the door to take a peek – for 25–30 minutes. The soufflé should be well risen. A skewer or a strand of spaghetti pushed quickly into the centre will confirm that it is cooked right through if it comes out without any runny mixture sticking to it (though the soufflé should be slightly wobbly, and definitely not solid). Serve immediately, with a tart leaf salad and a sprinkling of grated Cheddar or Parmesan.

Using up leftovers in soufflés...

Broccoli, leek, spinach or rocket Add a teacup of finely chopped cooked vegetables or uncooked rocket to the base mixture before folding in the whites. I always add an extra egg white to help hold the whole thing up (whisk it up with the rest). You could use Stilton here instead of other hard cheese.

Butternut squash or sweet potato Use a teacup of cooked vegetables cut into very small dice and a sprinkling of fresh thyme, adding them to the base mixture. Substitute goat's cheese for hard cheese, if you like, and add an extra egg white to the beaten whites.

Courgette Add to the base mixture a good teacupful of cooked grated courgettes, squeezed fairly dry, and season with lots of freshly ground black pepper. Add an extra egg white to the beaten whites.

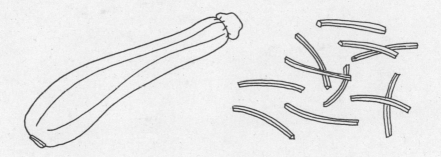

Making Simple Cheese

A litre of surplus milk is all you need for around 225g cottage cheese or a little less paneer, and both are as straightforward to make as yogurt. Cottage cheese is delicious in salads or savoury pancake fillings, while paneer can be eaten on its own or take the place of meat in Indian curries with tomatoes, spinach peas or almost any other vegetable. Both will keep in the fridge for up to a week in an airtight box (as with mozzarella, including a little of the watery whey will help to keep the cheeses fresh).

Cottage Cheese

I think full-fat milk is best here but skimmed will work too.

Bring 1 litre of milk to the boil in a large pan. Turn off the heat, add a tablespoon of lemon juice and a pinch of salt and stir well. After about 5 minutes the curds and whey (or watery fluid) will start to separate. When they are completely separate, strain the whole lot through a fine sieve or muslin bag and, while it is still in the sieve or bag, gently rinse the lumpy white curds under the tap to cool them down.

Push down on the curds in the sieve to squeeze out as much whey as possible. What's left is the best kind of cottage cheese.

Paneer

The Indian way with cottage cheese is to squeeze and press it quite hard until it forms a sliceable soft cheese. It is one of the great delights of Indian cooking, a sublimely gentle partner for vegetables in a subtle curry or eaten on its own with figs or dates, with a plate of fresh herbs or with a dollop of runny honey and some fresh walnuts or toasted nuts.

Make cottage cheese as above, then put the curds into a clean tea towel or a piece of muslin. Twist the cloth to wring out as much liquid as possible. You could also tie the ends together and leave the cheese suspended over a bowl to drip for a few hours. Put the cloth and curds on a plate, then put a heavy weight on top – a big can of tomatoes or a saucepan filled with water will do – slightly slanting the plate in the sink or another large bowl so that the last drops of whey can run off. After about 5 hours, the cheese will be done.

Salads

We tend to think of salads as using lots of the freshest ingredients, so they often get forgotten when it comes to leftovers. But salads are more than just about summer and dietary worthiness – with a handful of good fresh herbs or some toasted nuts or seeds, a simple plate of leaves with leftover meat, fish or vegetables is less an apologetic side dish than a meal in itself.

Leftover fish flaked with some roughly chopped tomatoes, a finely chopped shallot, some good black olives, a minced anchovy fillet and a garlicky dressing is not quite Niçoise, but it's just as deliciously filling. Home-made Paneer or Cottage Cheese (see page 206), with a handful of windowsill herbs torn over it, is virtually food for free as well as being good for you, while the last slice of bacon or even just its rind, quickly crisped up in a frying pan and crumbled over a salad of leftover boiled potatoes, transforms both humble ingredients into something really tasty. I've included some warm salads here too, as an alternative to green leaves – they are just brilliant for using up all sorts of languishing food.

Dressings made of oil and vinegar (or lemon juice) are great carriers for the added flavours of garlic, chopped herbs, mustard or even chilli. In general the ratio of oil to astringent should be three or four to one. Home-made mayonnaise also comes in handy – see page 34.

The Simplest Leftover Vegetable Salad

In the summer, when there are gluts of courgettes, beetroot, peppers, asparagus, French beans, new potatoes and so on (and when they are cheap in the shops), it's worth cooking a bit more than you need so that you can combine them all in a stunning leftover salad – what our eighteenth-century ancestors would have called a Russian salad.

Ideally, make this salad from a combination of all the vegetables mentioned above, each cooked until only just tender. Otherwise work with what you have to hand. You can also add your own roasted tomatoes or peppers (see page 44), or bottled artichoke hearts cut into large chunks. Arrange the cooked vegetables on a plate. If you've taken them from the fridge, leave them to reach room temperature.

Either use home-made mayonnaise for the dressing (see page 34) or make something more astringent by mixing 3 or 4 parts extra virgin olive oil to 1 part red wine vinegar. Add good coarse salt and a grinding of pepper to taste. Toss with the vegetables, check the seasoning, add fresh herbs to taste and serve with warm crusty bread, garlic-rubbed toast, toasted flatbreads or whatever you like best.

Roast Vegetable Salad with Shredded Meat

The principle here is to take any uncooked vegetables left in the fridge, toss them in olive oil and then roast them until they are cooked through (see page 102). The lovely thing is that the vegetable sugars caramelise, rather like the sticky, sweet outside of roast meat, adding punch to the flavour of your dish. If you are looking for inspiration, some of the combinations for roast vegetables on pages 102–3 will be helpful.

Rather than fresh leaves, the roast vegetables (served warm or tepid) form the bedrock of this salad, though you can add a few good salad leaves if you have them to hand. Then simply top the lot with a handful of meat per person and toss with your favourite dressing. You could also add some toasted nuts or seeds – sesame, pumpkin, pine nut and walnut are particularly good – or chopped herbs such as mint, coriander, parsley or basil. If you have chicken, duck or other poultry left over, I think it's best to pull it apart with your hands so that it shreds across its natural grain. Unlike the Christmas turkey, there's so little flesh on a duck that there's rarely enough of the deliciously dense meat left over for more than one person: what better reason to have lunch alone? Oh, and there's nothing stopping you from using this recipe for other kinds of meat or fish either.

Some ideas for different dressings...

Pesto Lovely with almost any poultry or fish – see page 139.

For leftover turkey Use 3 or 4 parts olive oil to 1 part white wine vinegar or tarragon vinegar, with a little Dijon mustard.

For duck Try a mixture of olive oil, sesame oil, a squeeze of lime, a dash of soy sauce and some chopped garlic and grated chilli (top tip: if you don't feel like chopping, deseeding or peeling chilli, ginger or garlic, you can rub them through a microplane grater – the skin and seeds will be left on top).

For chicken A classic dressing of 3 or 4 parts olive oil to 1 part balsamic vinegar, plus crushed garlic to taste and a pinch of dried mustard powder.

For beef Olive oil, a squeeze of lime and a little horseradish, over a base of roast potatoes.

For pork A classic combination with Bottled Roasted Peppers (see page 44). Add toasted pine nuts, capers and herbs to the salad before dressing with a simple vinaigrette blitzed with some Bottled Dried Tomatoes (see page 44).

For oily fish For mackerel or smoked salmon, use oil, lemon juice and a little horseradish or chopped dill. This is particularly nice on roast fennel or celery.

For lamb Use oil, lemon juice, chopped mint and/or ½ teaspoon of harissa. Roast parsnips and sweet potatoes would be lovely here.

For cheese Adding cheese to the salad, along with shredded meat or even instead of it, is a great way of using Cottage Cheese or Paneer (see page 206) or the ends of almost any cheese. Consider crumbling soft goat's cheese, ricotta or feta over the warm roast vegetables, or pare Parmesan or Cheddar into fine slices with a potato peeler. The best vinaigrette for cheese is a fruity olive oil and a drizzle of really rich aged balsamic vinegar, with a grinding of coarse black pepper and a scattering of sea salt.

You could also try...

Potted Christmas turkey As an alternative to serving strips of meat with a roast vegetable salad, you could 'pot' the meat and serve with separate salad leaves and crusty bread. Simply whiz up the leftover meat in a food processor with a good spoonful of butter, some salt and pepper and a squeeze of lemon juice to taste. The consistency should be not dry but moist, like a pâté. Put the mixture in a pot and chill before serving.

Two Eastern-Style Vegetable Salads

These two crunchy salads are real fridge clearers. You need only a handful of raw vegetables and another of bean sprouts or almonds to bring them brightly alive.

Gado Gado

This is a warm Indonesian salad made from strips of crunchy raw vegetables, such as mangetout, peppers and cucumber. You can also use up whatever vegetables you have lying around in the fridge – sliced finely or even grated – with strips of torn chicken or other poultry. Add bean sprouts for extra crunch. Serve with a slightly warm peanut sauce, either from a bottle or made by thinning 2 tablespoons of peanut butter with a little lime juice, a drop of Tabasco and a dessertspoon of water.

Pork and Noodle Salad

First cook some fine noodles, then drain and cool. Mix with minced leftover pork, grated carrot, shredded Chinese leaves or baby spinach, plus some chopped fresh mint and coriander. Flake some toasted almonds over the top and toss with a dressing of oil, a squeeze of lime, a dash of sesame oil and a pinch of dried chilli flakes.

Bread Salad

Known as *panzanella* in Italy, this is a traditional dish all around the Mediterranean and in the Middle East. It's more filling than your average salad and replete with the sunny flavours of ripe tomatoes, garlic, lemon and basil. You do have to use a staling baguette or ciabatta loaf, or some toasted Middle Eastern flatbread, because it simply won't work with British bread, needing a higher proportion of crunchy crust.

ripe red tomatoes
a stale baguette or ciabatta loaf, or lightly toasted Middle Eastern flatbread
garlic
lemon juice
basil leaves
good olive oil
balsamic or wine vinegar
salt and pepper

1

Chop as many tomatoes as you think you will eat into bite-sized pieces and put the whole lot, including seeds and juice, into a serving bowl.

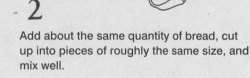

2

Add about the same quantity of bread, cut up into pieces of roughly the same size, and mix well.

3

Add some finely chopped garlic to taste, a good squeeze of lemon, a generous helping of chopped basil and a dressing made of 4 parts olive oil to 1 part vinegar. Turn the whole lot well. The salad should be wet but not sloppy, with enough juices to be soaked up by the bread, leaving none of it hard and dry. Cover with a clean tea towel and leave for a good hour before serving.

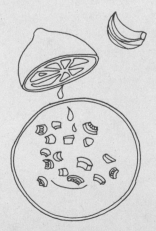

Two Leftover Beef Salads

The rarer the meat the better – don't bother with these salads if your meat is cooked through. For both salads, it's crucial to trim the meat of any fat and gristle and slice it as thinly as you possibly can.

An Italian Beef Salad

I make this salad a lot and generally buy a slightly larger piece of beef than we need, and hold back the very pinkest meat for the next day. Traditionally it is made from boiled beef but roast meat works just as well.

Serves 2

3 celery sticks or 1 fennel bulb, sliced extremely thinly
1–2 teacups (about 200g) leftover roast beef, sliced very finely
   into strips about 4 x 2cm
3 tablespoons good virgin olive oil
1 tablespoon wine vinegar or lemon juice
a pinch of sea salt
freshly ground black pepper

Arrange the celery or fennel on a large plate along with the thin slices of beef. Mix the olive oil with the vinegar or lemon juice and salt, then drizzle this over the salad. Finish with a good grinding of black pepper.

You could also try...

A drained can of white beans Warm the beans through just slightly in some of the olive oil and substitute for the fennel or celery.

An alternative dressing For a chunky salsa, roughly chop together parsley, capers, anchovies and a deseeded tomato. Thin with good olive oil and a little white wine vinegar and add a teaspoon of Dijon mustard. Drizzle over the salad. (You could also use Bagnetto as a dressing, see page 46.)

214

A Vietnamese Beef Salad

This is another way to use up leftover beef, provided it is pretty rare and tender, since the acid in the limes will continue to 'cook' it. It may sound odd but, trust me, the results are superb.

Serves 2

1 garlic clove, crushed
1 green or red chilli, deseeded and very finely chopped
2 tablespoons Thai fish sauce
1 tablespoon caster sugar
2 tablespoons lime juice (about 2 limes)
zest of 1 lime, finely shredded
1–2 teacups (about 200g) cooked beef, sliced into fine strips
  about 1cm wide

Combine all the ingredients except the beef in a mortar and work with the pestle to ensure that the garlic and chilli are well pounded and combined with the liquid. Allow to stand for about 20 minutes, until the sugar has dissolved.

Arrange the beef on a plate and pour over the dressing. Let it stand for 10 minutes and then serve.

You could add...

Tomato Deseeded and finely chopped, for colour and a new depth of flavour. Add to the finished salad and combine well with the beef.

Rare leftover lamb Omit the fish sauce from the dressing. Use lamb instead of beef and gently mix it with a finely sliced red onion, and/or a few finely chopped mint leaves – plus, if you have some, some really slim green beans that have been rapidly boiled, drained and cooled. Pour over the dressing, as above.

A Cupboard Salad
of Warm Pulses, Nuts and Cheese

This makes a filling meal on its own. I deliberately cook too many Puy lentils so that I can make the salad below, but you can vary things by using whatever canned pulses or beans you have in the cupboard, with the cheese and nuts of your choice. The salad doesn't have to be warm either, but the advantage of the heat is that it encourages the cheese to ooze.

Serves 2

2 teacups cooked Puy lentils
2 handfuls of rocket, baby spinach or other salad leaves
1 small goat's cheese, broken into chunks or sliced
a handful of walnuts, roughly chopped and toasted
a few roasted peppers (optional – see page 44)

For the dressing:
1 small garlic clove, crushed
a good pinch of sea salt
1 teaspoon dry mustard powder
1 tablespoon balsamic vinegar
1 tablespoon each of walnut oil and olive oil

Warm the lentils slightly and put them in a bowl. Mix all the ingredients for the dressing and toss with the lentils. Arrange the leaves on a plate and spoon over the lentil mixture. Add the goat's cheese, the toasted walnuts and, if you like, a few strips of roasted peppers. Serve immediately.

Some ideas for different combinations...

Chickpea and Parmesan Use a drained can of chickpeas in place of the lentils, warmed gently in a pan with a little olive oil, and substitute Parmesan shavings for the goat's cheese. Make a dressing of oil, lemon juice and crushed garlic. Leave out the nuts.

216

Chorizo and chickpea Substitute a drained can of chickpeas for the lentils, warming them gently in a little olive oil. Thinly slice some cooked chorizo or skin it and crumble it over the leaves and chickpeas. Use a dressing of olive oil and red wine vinegar. Leave out the nuts and use some Parmesan shavings instead of goat's cheese to serve.

Leftover chicken Shredded leftover chicken can be added to any warmed pulses. Use either the dressing in the main recipe opposite or a mixture of oil, lemon juice and crushed garlic. Toasted pine nuts are good here.

Leftover fish Particularly good with warm Puy lentils. In this case, I would use a very simple dressing of 3 parts olive oil to 2 parts balsamic vinegar, omit the cheese and use toasted pine nuts instead of walnuts.

Potato Salad,
Several Ways

The simplest potato salads, made with cold boiled potatoes, need not be gloopy or heavy, though it is important to use waxy potatoes, such as Charlottes or Jersey Royals, as floury ones will crumble. Dress with a good mayonnaise, either from a bottle or home-made (see page 34), or a light, citrussy vinaigrette, and finish with the zing and fragrance of chopped fresh herbs. Potato salads are great on their own or with smoked or pickled fish, but they also go particularly well with cured meats such as salami, prosciutto, jamon serrano, chorizo or good English ham.

Mint and chervil I'm always inclined to warm leftover boiled potatoes just a little in the microwave before making this salad, as they are best tepid – the gentle heat intensifies the flavour of the herbs. Slice the warm potatoes into a bowl and add a little finely sliced raw shallot or spring onion and finely chopped mint and chervil. Season with crunchy salt such as Maldon and drizzle over some good olive oil mixed with a little Dijon mustard and a splash of wine vinegar or lemon juice.

With fennel Finely slice fennel and fry in a little oil until golden and tender. Mix with sliced boiled potatoes, season and dress with olive oil and a squeeze of lemon juice. Black olives or capers go well with this.

White bean, apple and chicory Use a can of drained white beans mixed with sliced boiled potatoes, finely sliced raw chicory and some chunks of sharp dessert apple. Make a dressing of 3 or 4 parts olive oil to 1 part white wine vinegar and season with salt and pepper.

Greek style Finely slice a small red onion and a garlic clove and mix with sliced boiled potatoes and chunks of ripe tomato. Lightly scatter chopped parsley on top and toss in a dressing made of 4 parts olive oil and 1 part red wine vinegar, with lots of sea salt and black pepper.

Spanish style This is a warm salad. Fry good chunks of leftover boiled potatoes in oil until golden, adding a couple of chopped garlic cloves right at the end. You could add ½ finely chopped red chilli, if you like. Put the whole lot into a serving bowl and pour over a dressing of 4 parts olive oil to 1 part good balsamic vinegar. Season and add a handful of chopped basil, if you have it. Serve warm.

French style Mix sliced cold boiled potatoes with a few of the tenderest little thyme leaves, stripped from their stem, or with chopped parsley and chives. Make a dressing of 4 parts olive oil to 1 part white wine vinegar, adding a little crushed garlic, some Dijon mustard and some salt and pepper.

Russian style Mix chunks of cold boiled potato with diced cucumber and beetroot. Add slices of hard-boiled egg, a teaspoon or so of rinsed capers and some sliced spring onions. If you have it, chopped dill is lovely with this salad. The dressing should be plain soured cream seasoned with salt and pepper.

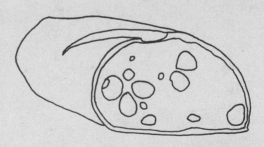

Things to do
with Bread

Of all the food we throw away, bread makes up the largest amount (over 516,000 tonnes of it a year, worth over £750 million) – which is perhaps not entirely surprising when you discover that in the UK around 12 million loaves are sold *each day*. Whether you buy a pre-packed sliced white loaf from the supermarket or bread from your local baker, or whether you make it yourself, you don't have to throw away the end of the loaf. For a start, you can store it in the freezer as breadcrumbs (see page 49) for using with meatballs, fishcakes and stuffings or as the crispy top for bakes.

Bread or rolls going stale can be given a new lease of life by swooshing them briefly under cold running water. They should be wet all over but not soggy. Put them into a medium oven (180°C/Gas Mark 4) for 5 minutes and, hey presto, they will be crusty and fresh again. You really can't do this more than once with the same piece of bread.

All that aside, there are also several delicious puddings to make with either sliced bread or breadcrumbs. Part of a brilliant British tradition of almost forgotten 'nursery' dishes, these include classics such as summer pudding – the dessert that, like Marmite, divides the nation into lovers and haters.

Eggy Bread

Also known as French toast, this is lovely for a weekend breakfast instead of pancakes. We eat it with sliced bananas and some crisp bacon, with a little lump of melting butter and a good gloop of maple syrup: it's a sweet-salty indulgence. You could serve yours with far more sophisticated cream and blueberries, peaches or any other juicy fruit, or make a savoury version by leaving out the sugar and adding a little grated cheese to the mix.

Serves 2 adults, or 1 adult and 2 young children

2 large eggs
1 teaspoon caster sugar
2 tablespoons cream or milk
butter for frying
4 medium-thick slices of semi-stale white bread, crusts and all
    (stale brioche is also sometimes used, but I never have that
    kind of thing just lying around)

Whisk the eggs, sugar and cream or milk together in a shallow dish. Melt a knob of butter in a large frying pan until softly foaming. Dunk the slices of bread into the egg mixture one by one, making sure that each slice is well covered and beginning to soak up the egg, then gently put them in the hot frying pan. Fry on both sides over a medium heat until crisp and golden.

Two Iconic Puddings

These puddings were probably favourites of your grandmother and her mother before her. One is sweet and warming for winter, layered with dried fruit; the other relies on the tang of summer berries.

Bread and Butter Pudding

In this dish, the crunch of the bread at the top is offset by a creamy, sweet custard. There are lots of ways of varying it to include different dried fruits. You could also make it in teacups for individual puddings, which look fantastic and make everyone feel special. In this case, reduce the cooking time to 20–25 minutes.

Serves 4

2 tablespoons brandy or whisky – or fruit juice, if you prefer
100g raisins
200ml whole milk
100ml double cream
3 large eggs
100g sugar – caster or soft brown is best
250g staling white bread (you can also use brioche,
    panettone or any leftover bready thing), sliced
40g butter

If using alcohol, put it in a small pan with the raisins, bring to a simmer, then turn off the heat and allow to soak for a couple of hours. Otherwise, leave the fruit to soak in fruit juice.

To make the custard, put the milk and cream into a pan and bring to simmering point. Beat the eggs and sugar together in a bowl and then gradually pour the milk mixture on to them, whisking all the time so that you don't get scrambled egg. Set aside.

Butter the bread and cut it into triangles or squares. Arrange a layer of bread butter-side up in a buttered ovenproof dish. Sprinkle on some of the raisins with a little of the alcohol or juice and continue layering the ingredients in this way until you have about 3 layers. Pour over the custard and leave to sit for 30 minutes.

Preheat the oven to 180°C/Gas Mark 4. Place the dish in a roasting tin containing enough boiling water to come half way up the sides of the dish, then bake for 30–40 minutes; it will be ready when crisp on top and slightly resilient (rather than sloppy) to the touch.

To change things about...

Marmalade Spread this on the bread and butter before making up the dish.

Other dried fruits Chopped dried apricots or mango are great substitutes for the raisins.

Nutella and pears Spread the bread with butter and chocolate spread before making up the dish. Replace the raisins with peeled, cored and sliced pears.

Cold chocolate bread and butter pudding This is an adaptation of a classic Delia Smith recipe. Use thick white bread slices and omit the raisins. Melt 150g dark chocolate and stir it into the custard. Continue as above and serve chilled.

Summer Pudding

The trick with this pudding is to pack it full of really juicy fruit and weight it heavily. Then be patient. Leave it for a good day so that the bread can suck up all those amazing juices as the weights pack it down tightly.

If you have a garden full of summer fruits, that's ideal. I almost always buy a pack of frozen summer fruits from the supermarket and they do have the advantage of loads of juice. I make this pudding with wild blackberries in late September but sometimes find they aren't quite tart enough to match the blandness of the bread; a squeeze of lemon juice can remedy this.

Serves 6

750g mixed fresh or frozen berries and currants (strawberries, raspberries, redcurrants, blackcurrants and blackberries are all good)
140g caster sugar
a little butter
a small white loaf, sliced and with crusts removed (the bread can be stale, but should not be stiff)

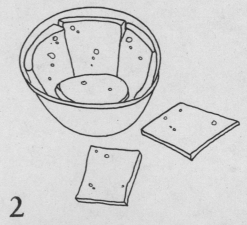

1

Put the fruit and sugar in a pan over a low heat and cook until the juices just begin to flow. Set to one side to cool.

2

Lightly butter an 850–900ml glass or ceramic bowl. Cut a disk of bread to fit the base and then line the sides with slices of bread, pressing them in firmly and leaving absolutely no gaps. Overlaps are fine.

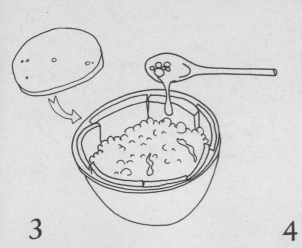

3

Spoon all the fruit into the bowl along with about three-quarters of the juice (reserve the rest of the juice for later). Cover the top with a slice of bread, cut to fit.

4

Find a plate or saucer that fits just inside the rim of the bowl, put it on top of the pudding and weight it down with a bag of sugar, some cans or the weights from old-fashioned scales. Leave the pudding in the fridge or in a cool pantry, if you have one, all day or overnight.

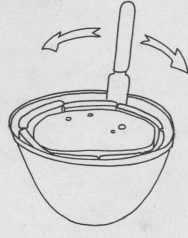

5

To serve, remove the weights and the plate. Run a blunt knife carefully around the inside of the bowl.

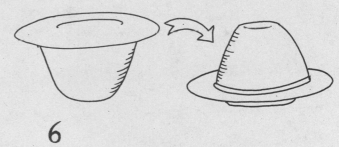

6

Put a serving plate over the top of the bowl and, holding on firmly, invert it all. If the juices have saturated all the bread, the pudding should plop out easily.

7

Pour the reserved juice over the pudding, being sure to cover any white patches of bread, and serve with cream, vanilla ice cream or mascarpone.

Two Puddings Using Breadcrumbs

These are old-fashioned puddings that really deserve rediscovery. They are both a brilliant way of using up stale bread in the form of crumbs and both are served hot – delicious with vanilla ice cream or home-made Custard (see page 33).

Fruit Charlotte

Charlottes are in some ways a moulded variation on Brown Betty (see page 228) and are another languishing 'nursery' pudding in which fruit is layered with breadcrumbs. You can use any fruit you like in place of the apples, stewing it first with a little sugar to taste. Rhubarb is fantastic with a little ginger and brown sugar, or mix it with raspberries. My brother loved pineapple Charlotte when we were small and it is seriously good with the tart addition of redcurrants. Ripe summer stone fruit and sweetened autumn plums are both equally inviting.

Serves 4

4–6 slices of bread, lightly buttered, crusts removed
450g apples (a mixture of Bramleys and Cox's is good),
   peeled, cored and diced
50g raisins or currants
1 tablespoon caster or raw cane sugar
30g butter, plus a little extra for frying
1 egg
120g breadcrumbs
1 teaspoon ground cinnamon

Butter a 600ml pudding basin or soufflé dish and line it with the slices of lightly buttered bread, reserving one for the top (if you prefer, you can

226

make a lighter dish by pressing breadcrumbs on to the sides of the basin but this is far more fiddly).

Put the apples, dried fruit, sugar and butter in a pan with a sprinkling of water and heat gently until the apples form a pulp. Leave to cool, then whisk the egg into the mix.

Preheat the oven to 180°C/Gas Mark 4. Mix the breadcrumbs with the cinnamon. Heat a little butter in a frying pan, add the breadcrumb mixture and cook until crisp and lightly coloured. You will need to stir pretty constantly and watch to check the bread does not burn.

Pour a third of the apple pulp into the basin, top with half the toasted breadcrumbs and repeat in layers, finishing with a layer of apple. Top with a final slice of buttered bread, cutting it to fit and making sure the filling is well covered. Cover with foil and bake for half an hour. Remove the foil and bake for a further 15 minutes, until the crust is browning. Remove from the oven and leave to rest for 10 minutes, then run a knife around the edge and invert the pudding on to a serving plate. Serve warm with cream, ice cream, crème fraîche or Custard (see page 33).

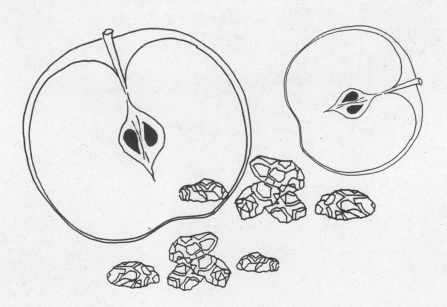

Brown Betty

This pudding used to be heavy with suet and steamed for hours – until it evolved into something significantly lighter. Almost any fruit can be used in place of the apples, including pineapple, mango or even rhubarb when it's in season. You could also replace some of the apple with dried fruit, such as currants or raisins.

Serves 4

60g stale breadcrumbs
1 tablespoon melted butter, plus a little butter for greasing the dish
130g soft brown sugar
1 teaspoon ground cinnamon
1 teaspoon ground nutmeg or mixed spice
a pinch of salt
juice and grated zest of 1 lemon
1 teaspoon vanilla extract
400g apples (preferably cooking apples), peeled, cored and diced

Preheat the oven to 180°C/Gas Mark 4. Butter a 1-litre baking dish. Mix the breadcrumbs with the melted butter. In a separate bowl, mix the sugar with the spices, salt, lemon zest and vanilla.

Spread about a third of the buttery crumbs over the bottom of your dish. Cover with a layer of half the apples, then half the spicy sugar mixture. Sprinkle half the lemon juice and 2 tablespoons of water on top. Then start the process again with another third of the crumbs, the remaining apples and then the last of the sugar. Sprinkle lemon juice and 2 tablespoons of water over it again and finish with the remaining crumbs on the top. Cover with foil and bake for 40 minutes. Remove the foil and increase the heat to 200°C/Gas Mark 6. Bake for 10 minutes to get a crispy top. Serve with cream, Custard (see page 33) or vanilla ice cream.

Fruit Past its Best

I don't think the kitchen fruit bowl existed in my childhood – it seems to be a particularly modern invention, perhaps a result of the five-a-day mantra. Some fruit, it's true, is best kept out of the fridge, and to some extent that's a matter of choice. But there's no doubt that most of us buy far more fruit than we actually eat, and that much of it goes mouldy in front of our eyes. To take the simple apple as an example, we throw away 4.4 million *each and every day* – at a cost of around £317 million per year. Shocking, eh?

Some of the following recipes can be made with fruit in its prime, too. If you are juicing, for instance, you should use only firm, ripe fruit. Smoothies and lollies, however, are much tastier made with really ripe fruit, and banana cake can be made only with bananas that are going black.

For crumbles, baked or stewed fruit, don't forget delicious home-made custard – the recipe is on page 33.

If you're looking for fruit pies, turn to pages 130–2; for bready-fruity puddings, see pages 224–9; for baking with fruit, see pages 241–6.

Smoothies and Milkshakes

Smoothies (made with fruit juice or yogurt) and milkshakes (made with milk or ice cream) are so straightforward that to give a recipe seems almost superfluous. If you want something really cold, you can add ice to either and blitz it up along with everything else. Soft fruits such as berries and stone fruit can be blended with milk, yogurt or ice cream. A liquidiser is best, but you could use a 'stick' blender or even a food processor. Use a juicer for citrus fruits and a juice extractor for fruits such as apples, melons and pineapples, adding this juice to the liquidiser with the other ingredients.

For any smoothie or milkshake, including all the suggestions below, you will need to blend the fruit a little before adding milk, yogurt, ice cream or juice to make a really smooth drink. Play around with the amounts of liquid or ice cream until you find the strength and texture you like best. Drink immediately. Here are some mouth-watering combinations:

- Banana with a squirt of runny honey or a scoop of chocolate ice cream
- Cherry and apple or apricot
- Mango and the pulp of a passion fruit
- Mango and banana
- Peach and raspberry
- Pear, melon and cucumber – add mint leaves, if you like
- Pineapple, strawberry and mango
- Pineapple and raspberry, strawberry or banana
- Pineapple and mint leaves, blended with ice

Smoothie and milkshake mixtures are also great for freezing into ice lollies. Use a little less milk or fruit juice to make them quite strongly fruity. For a change, use plain yogurt and fruit (but if you are using berries, sieve the mixture before freezing if you don't want your kids to complain).

Granitas and Sorbets

Sorbets and granitas are both sweetened fruit ices that can easily be made at home, but while sorbets are smooth, sweetened with a sugar syrup, granitas are chunkier and 'icier', a bit like a carnival slush puppy but without the lurid colour. For both, any of the fruits or combinations suggested for smoothies and milkshakes on the previous page will work supremely well, as will ripe melon, grapefruit, pears or oranges.

A Basic Granita

I think the crunchiness of granita works best with citrus fruits such as oranges, lemons and grapefruits. Pineapple and passion fruit also have the right kind of tartness, as do berries like redcurrants, strawberries and early raspberries. If the fruit you are using is very sweet, add a squeeze of lemon juice. Vary the exact amount of water and sugar to fruit according to your taste – these are only guidelines.

Serves 4

3–4 teacups (around 400g) prepared fruit, or 800ml–1 litre
*   *freshly squeezed citrus juice*
175g caster sugar, or to taste
about 570ml water
a squeeze of lemon juice (optional)

If using prepared fruit, blend it in a liquidiser, add sugar to taste and blend again. Add water (to taste, but the mixture needs to be quite liquid) and blend once more. Strain through a nylon sieve.

If using juice, simply mix it with the sugar and water, adding a squeeze of lemon if the juice is very sweet.

Freeze in the widest plastic box you have for 2 hours. Take it out of the freezer and thoroughly mash up the icy crystals with a fork. Freeze for another hour, break up with a fork again and then serve in glasses.

A Basic Sorbet

You can ring the changes with sorbets by replacing the syrup with a tub of crème fraîche or even yogurt. These will give creamier results, somewhere between a classic clear sorbet and an ice cream, and work best with tart berry fruits such as redcurrants or raspberries. If you have a leftover egg white, whisk it up and fold it into your fruity mixture for extra lightness.

Serves 4

125g caster sugar
125ml water
3–4 teacups (about 400g) prepared soft fruit
a squeeze of lemon juice (optional)

To make a sugar syrup, put the sugar and water in a small pan and stir over a moderate heat until the sugar has dissolved. Simmer gently for a minute, then allow to cool.

Whiz the prepared fruit in a blender, then strain the pulp though a nylon sieve, pushing it through with the back of a wooden spoon. For very sweet fruit, such as pears, you might like to add a squeeze of lemon juice to brighten (but not overwhelm) the flavour.

Mix the fruit pulp with some of the syrup, tasting as you go. The last thing you want is for your sorbet to be really sweet, but bear in mind that freezing intensifies the sharpness of the fruit, so err slightly on the side of sweetness.

If you have an ice-cream maker, it will now come into its own. Alternatively, pour the mixture into the widest plastic box you own. Put it in the freezer and, when it is set quite firm (but not hard), remove it and whisk vigorously. This breaks down the ice crystals and makes for a smoother sorbet. Repeat the freezing and whisking routine a couple of times for the best effect before storing the sorbet in a plastic tub (such as an old ice-cream container) in the freezer. Take it out of the freezer 15 minutes or so before you want to serve it.

Four Simple Ways
with Fruit

These four ideas are almost afterthoughts in any kitchen – the bare minimum, if you like, that you can do to turn something on its way towards the bin into something more than worth eating.

Dried Fruit

Dried fruit keeps for ages in an airtight container and is great for lunchboxes, picnics and afternoon snacks. Like Bottled Dried Tomatoes (see page 44), the flavour becomes deep and luxurious.

Apple, pineapple, mango, apricot and pear all work well. Peel the fruit if necessary, core or stone it, then cut it into slim rings or slices. If you like the crunch and sparkle of sugar, you could scatter a little caster sugar over the slices before baking them. Soft spices like ground cinnamon and mixed spice are all good too.

Spread the sliced fruit out on a baking tray and place in a very low oven – around 100°C or the lowest possible gas mark. Rather than crisp up, the fruit should dry slowly, its sugars concentrating as it shrinks slightly. Depending on the fruit you use and how thickly you cut it, this can take anything from 45 minutes to a couple of hours. Allow to cool before storing.

Fruit Fritters

This is a time-honoured way of dealing with ripening fruit. Make up the pancake batter on pages 196–7. Heat a good centimetre of vegetable oil in a wide pan and, when it is shimmering but not smoking, dip chunks of peeled apple, pear or even banana into the batter and slip them carefully into the hot fat. Fry until puffed up and golden, then drain on kitchen paper and sprinkle over a little caster sugar to serve.

Caramelised Fruit

Caramelised ripe fruit is lovely in pancakes or served with yogurt or ice cream. Caramelising is a brilliant thing to do with bananas in particular but apples, pears, mangoes, pineapple and oranges are all delicious too. Exact quantities don't really matter. Simply melt equal quantities of butter and caster sugar in a frying pan – gently, so that neither burn – stirring occasionally. Once the sugar has dissolved into a caramel, add chopped fruit and shake it around in the pan until it is well covered in its gooey sauce. Let it cook over a low heat until the fruit is tender – bananas will take almost no time, while apples will need around 7 minutes. How soft you let the fruit become is up to you. Allow to cool just a little before serving, or dollop a good spoonful of ice cream over the fruit as you serve. Watch for children's mouths: fudgy, molten sugar is incredibly hot.

Stewed Fruit

Almost any fruit (apart from bananas) can be stewed into a compote with sugar to taste. Adding a sweetly crunchy top turns it into a crumble; swirling it cold into cream transforms it into a fool. Or you could use it to flavour plain yogurt for breakfast. It will keep in the fridge for up to a week and freezes brilliantly.

The general principle is easy. Simply peel, core or stone and dice whatever fruit you want to use. Put it into a heavy-bottomed pan with caster sugar to taste and a scant sprinkling of water (by which I mean a teaspoon or two only). Cook very, very gently until the fruit collapses into a soft, juicy pulp, but watch that it doesn't catch and burn on the bottom of the pan, stirring occasionally and adding a little more water if it looks very dry.

Try playing with gentle spices or herbs according to the fruit. For instance, cinnamon, nutmeg, mace or rosemary are lovely with apples or pears, vanilla seeds or thyme leaves with summer stone fruit; star anise or mint leaves take pineapple to a new dimension; rhubarb loves ginger and brown sugar and autumn plums like brown sugar too.

A Fruit Crumble

All crumbles use stewed fruit as their base but you need only to soften the fruit a little and get the juices running, rather than reduce it to a pulp, or you will lose the bite and body of the dish. Blackberry and apple in combination is, I suppose, the dish of my imaginary desert island, but plain apple comes a close second, along with rhubarb or gooseberries when they're in season.

It's best not to over-sweeten the stewed fruit, so that it cuts through the sweetness of the crumble. If you are using apples, always go for cookers – dessert apples rarely have the slightly sour edge you need. Serve crumbles with home-made Custard (page 33) or a whirl of whipped cream or vanilla ice cream to balance the heat and the crunch.

Serves 4

600–800g fruit, prepared and just lightly stewed with caster sugar (see page 235), so that it softens without entirely losing its shape

For the crumble:
200g plain flour
a pinch of salt
100g unsalted butter from the fridge, diced
100g caster sugar – or muscovado,
 if you want a deeper, richer flavour

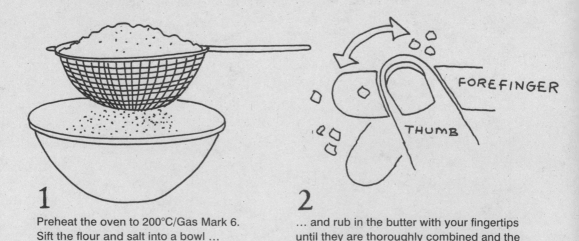

FOREFINGER

THUMB

1
Preheat the oven to 200°C/Gas Mark 6. Sift the flour and salt into a bowl …

2
… and rub in the butter with your fingertips until they are thoroughly combined and the mixture resembles very fine breadcrumbs.

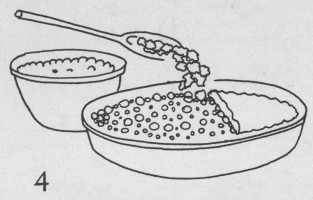

3

Stir in the sugar.

4

Put the stewed fruit into an ovenproof dish and spoon over the crumble.

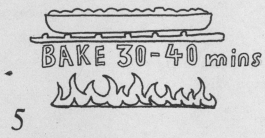

5

Bake for 30–40 minutes, until golden and bubbling around the edges.

To change things around a bit...

Use ginger nuts or digestive biscuits Blitzed into crumbs, biscuits can be used instead of flour and sugar. Mix roughly with the butter to make an alternative crumble.

Add nuts A handful is enough, chopped roughly to give the crumble crunch. Flaked almonds, walnuts and pecans are particularly nice.

Enrich the crumble Add a dessertspoon or so of cream – not to make a dough, just to moisten it.

Top the fruit with meringue instead Follow the meringue recipe on page 199 and spoon it over the fruit. Bake at 150°C/Gas Mark 2 for 30–40 minutes, until the meringue is colouring and hardening. I like to make these in small ramekins rather than one large dish. Serve hot or cold.

Fools

Like trifle, fools are burdened with a name of inconsequentiality and, well, foolishness. Loved since the Elizabethan period, they represent the essence of British summer. Gooseberries, apples and rhubarb are absolute classics but any Stewed Fruit (see page 235) will do. Make sure you let the cooked fruit cool completely before mixing it with the cream.

Strawberries and raspberries are also particularly good in fools but they don't need to be cooked first. Put them in a bowl, scatter over a little caster sugar and a teaspoon of thick, rich balsamic vinegar and allow them to sit for at least an hour. Pour off some juice and reserve it if there seems to be a lot, then mash the fruit roughly with a fork. Sounds odd, I know, but I promise that it won't taste too vinegary or acidic.

To make a fool, the ratio of softly whipped cream (or thick plain yogurt, if you prefer) to fruit should be about 2:1, but the exact quantities don't matter. Taste as you go along, adding more cream or fruit until you have the ideal balance of tartness to cream. The fruit should be folded in gently, letting it marble the cream rather than blend entirely into it.

For a complete change, make a fruit 'snow' instead of a fool, using stiffly beaten egg white rather than cream or yogurt. Apple snow is a very old dish, originally served with a sprig of rosemary.

Baked Fruit

Almost any kind of fruit can be baked in a ceramic dish with a little sugar, some gentle spices such as cinnamon, vanilla or star anise, plus a gloop of alcohol if there aren't kids involved. You'll get the same intensity of flavour as with stewed fruits, but in these dishes the fruit is designed not to fall apart but to hold its shape.

Apples, pears, peaches and even Christmas gluts of clementines, mandarins or satsumas all bake well, so here's a general recipe for baking fruit, along with plenty of taste combinations to inspire.

Baked Apples

There's almost nothing more satisfying than baked apples, served with home-made Custard (see page 33) or with leftover Christmas brandy butter. You can use either cooking or eating apples, though I prefer the sharpness of cookers.

Preheat the oven to 180°C/Gas Mark 4. Butter a baking dish just large enough to hold the apples quite tightly. Core (but don't peel) some small Bramley apples, then score round the circumference of each apple with a sharp knife to prevent them bursting. Fill up the cavity with raisins or sultanas. Squeeze some runny honey into each hole, or sprinkle on some soft brown sugar. Scatter over the dish a few knobs of butter, a little more brown sugar, plus a dessertspoon of water or cider for each apple. Bake for 40–50 minutes, until the apples are completely tender but not falling apart, with the juices sticky in the bottom of the dish.

Alternative combinations...

Spiced apples Add a little grating of nutmeg, a cinnamon stick or a pinch of ground cinnamon, or the seeds scraped from a vanilla pod to the filling mixture, to spice and subtly scent the apples. Cloves, if you like them, are also good in moderation.

Dessert apples and Calvados Halve and core each apple and place in a baking dish, cut-side up. Scatter over brown sugar and dot with butter. Add a dessertspoon of Calvados for each apple. Bake for 40 minutes, basting occasionally.

Pineapple This is a great way of using up a pineapple that's past its best, so long as the flesh is not browning. Peel, core and slice it and lay it in a buttered dish. Add a bruised stick of lemongrass, a kaffir lime leaf and a squeeze of lime juice, then scatter sugar over it and bake for 20 minutes or so, until tender. Serve with a little finely chopped mint or basil and some vanilla ice cream.

More baked fruit...

Christmas satsumas, clementines or similar First blanch the whole fruit in rapidly boiling water for 30 seconds to remove its bitterness, then drain. Poke a hole through the middle of each one and push in a star anise and a stick of cinnamon. Place in a dish and spoon a tablespoon of Cointreau or whisky over each one and sprinkle a little caster sugar on top. Bake as on the previous page for around 30 minutes, until tender. Serve whole, and use a teaspoon to scoop out the cooked flesh. If you prefer, you can omit the initial blanching and peel the fruit instead.

Peaches, nectarines or apricots Stone and quarter the fruit and lay it in a buttered dish. Sprinkle a tablespoon of Amaretto over each fruit, add a pinch of ground cinnamon or a vanilla pod (or a teaspoon of good vanilla extract) and bake for about 20 minutes, until tender. Discard the vanilla pod, if using, and serve with crème fraîche and macaroons.

Stone fruit with redcurrant jelly and meringue Halve the fruit and lay it cut-side up in a buttered dish. Put a teaspoon of redcurrant jelly in the centre of each half and top with meringue mix (see page 199). Bake for 20–30 minutes at 150°C/Gas Mark 2, until the meringue is crisp and just colouring.

Pears Halve and core the fruit and place in a buttered dish. Spoon over a tablespoon of Marsala or sweet sherry, push a couple of cinnamon sticks amongst the fruit and bake for 20 minutes or so, until tender. Serve with a bare scattering of dried lavender or a little chopped fresh thyme.

Plums Plums always become more tart as they cook, so you will almost certainly need a fair bit of sugar, but don't overdo it. Halve and stone the plums, place in a buttered dish and scatter soft brown sugar on top, then drizzle with a little Amaretto or port. Bake for about 20 minutes, until the juices start to run and the plums soften. Taste them and add a little more sugar if required. Serve with toasted flaked almonds scattered on top – the slight bitterness of the almonds works wonders and their crunch does heavenly battle with the melting flesh of the fruit.

Three Ways of Baking with Fruit

These three recipes are all vaguely 'cakey' and will give you an impressive pudding, a gooey cake for tea or picnics, or muffins galore for office lunches, school packs or general snacking. Banana cake is a law unto itself but the sponge pudding and muffins are, as usual, endlessly adaptable depending on what you need to use up.

Each of these recipes is also easy enough to make with the kids; I know where my eggs come from and have no hesitation about letting them scrape out the mixing bowl, which always seems, to me, one of the best parts of baking *en famille*.

Muffins

It's odd that muffins – so much more an American than a British tradition – tend to be overlooked as a magnificent and easy way to use up fruit. Even better, though it may seem odd to find a recipe for them in this chapter, savoury muffins use up cheese and leftover vegetables – fantastic for lunchboxes or picnics and pretty damn good for a grown-up desk lunch with, if you have it, a little chutney on the side.

In general, the trick is to mix muffin batter as little as possible, not worrying about a lump here or there (which also makes them ideal for kids to make).

This recipe makes quite a few muffins, especially if you decide to use mini-muffin tins instead of large ones, and they freeze brilliantly. To reheat them, wrap them in foil and put in a low oven (around 150°C/ Gas Mark 2) for 10 minutes or so.

Rather than fiddling around with muffin papers, you could use a well-greased rubber or tin muffin tray – but papers do help keep the muffins moist.

Makes 10–12

225g plain flour
1 teaspoon baking powder
1 teaspoon bicarbonate of soda
100g caster sugar (for fruit muffins), or 2 teaspoons caster sugar
    (for savoury muffins)
1 large egg, lightly beaten
60g unsalted butter, melted and cooled
150ml milk

For fruit muffins:
about 125g fruit, plus a handful of chopped nuts, if you like them

For savoury muffins:
about 125g raw or leftover cooked vegetables, and
    up to 60g grated cheese, along with a pinch of salt and
    a grinding of black pepper

Preheat the oven to 190°C/Gas Mark 5. Sift all the dry ingredients into a bowl and add your chosen fruit or vegetables, plus any other dry flavourings. In a separate bowl, lightly whisk together the egg, butter and milk. Add the egg mix to the dry ingredients and quickly stir everything together. It should have a thick 'dropping' consistency; if it seems too stiff, add a splash more milk – but *do not overwork the mixture.*

Dollop the batter into muffin cases, filling them about two-thirds full. Bake in the centre of the oven for 15–20 minutes (less if you are using mini-muffin tins), until risen and golden. Leave in the tins until cool enough to handle, then transfer to a wire rack.

There are lots of variations...

Blackberries or raspberries These are each delightful, and taste so much better (I think) than blueberries, with that same dark staining through the muffin. You could add the grated zest of an orange or lemon, which is particularly good with raspberries.

Banana Use very ripe bananas, mash them with a fork and add a squeeze of lemon and another of runny honey. A pinch of ground cinnamon also works well. When cooked, sprinkle poppy seeds on top.

Peach, nectarine or apricot Cut the fruit into small dice. Add a scraping of vanilla pod seeds or a pinch of ground cinnamon to the mix.

Grated apple Use 1 large or 2 small eating apples, peeled and grated, plus a teaspoon of ground cinnamon and about 60g raisins, sultanas or chopped dates.

Some ideas for savoury muffins...

Broccoli Cut leftover broccoli into small florets or dice and add about 60g mature Cheddar cheese, grated.

Carrot Use coarsely grated carrot plus 60g mature Cheddar cheese, grated. A small handful of pumpkin seeds and a tablespoon of chopped fresh coriander would be nice here too.

Courgette Grate courgettes that would otherwise languish in the fridge. Add an extra egg, ricotta cheese, broken into small pieces, and a few chopped chives, if you have them.

Peas Leftover peas are lovely with grated Parmesan.

Pumpkin Grate the flesh. Add a teaspoon of ground cinnamon and 30g chopped dates. Use soft brown sugar and add an extra egg for lightness.

Spinach Cooked, squeezed, cooled and chopped. Add a tablespoon of Onion Marmalade (see page 42). Grate Parmesan over the top of the muffins as they come out of the oven.

Ham and cheese Use 50g grated mature Cheddar cheese, ½ teacup of finely chopped cooked ham and a teaspoon of wholegrain or smooth mustard. A few chopped sage leaves or chives would also be nice here.

Sponge Pudding
for Ripe Stone Fruit or Rhubarb

My mum made this a lot when we were children. The fruit sinks into the cake mixture, leaving a craggy top and a moist, sticky underneath. You can whiz it all up with a hand whisk and then pretty much forget about it as it cooks. It looks and tastes as good as any bought pâtisserie for Sunday lunch with friends.

This pudding is equally tasty with the tartness of spring rhubarb or with ripe peaches, nectarines, apricots or even pears, but don't be tempted to use unripe fruit. If you find that the fruit sinks right to the bottom while it cooks – as it will sometimes do – the taste will still be fabulous and in some ways it can be an advantage: with the fruit playing hide-and-seek, the cake looks plain and uninspiring, until you cut into it.

Serves 4

about 500g rhubarb, nectarines, peaches or apricots
110g caster sugar, plus extra for sweetening the fruit
110g butter, at room temperature
2 large eggs
110g self-raising flour, sifted
1 teaspoon vanilla extract
a pinch of salt
a little milk or water
icing sugar, for dusting

Preheat the oven to 190°C/Gas Mark 5. To prepare the fruit, slice rhubarb into 2.5cm lengths or stone and slice peaches, nectarines or apricots. If the fruit is tart (and rhubarb will be), sprinkle caster sugar over it (you'll need a good 3 tablespoons for rhubarb).

Make the base of the pudding as you would a standard sponge. First beat the sugar and butter together until pale and fluffy. Lightly whisk the eggs in a separate bowl and then beat them slowly into the sugary butter, including a spoonful of the flour with the final addition to prevent them curdling. Add the vanilla. Sift the flour and salt from a good height into the bowl and lightly fold them in. If necessary, add a little milk or water to give the mixture a good dropping consistency – i.e. make it a mixture that will only just drop off a spoon.

Scrape the mixture into a well-buttered 20cm cake tin – ideally, a springform or loose-bottomed tin, which will help when turning the cake out. Drop the fruit gently all over the mixture. Bake for 40 minutes, until cooked right through (a metal skewer or a strand of raw spaghetti inserted into the centre should come out clean). Remove from the oven and allow to cool slightly in the tin.

Dust with icing sugar and serve warm, with cream or ice cream and some sliced fresh fruit, if you have it. Last time I made this pudding I used apricots for the cake and served it with a bowl of fresh mango – the pairing was delicious.

To ring the changes...

Baked custard Place a couple of teacups of very ripe prepared fruit in an ovenproof dish. Replace the sponge mix entirely with Custard (see page 33) and pour this over the fruit. Put the dish in a roasting tin containing enough hot water to come half way up the sides of the dish. Bake at 160°C/Gas Mark 3 for 15–20 minutes, until the custard has set. You could make this in individual ramekins instead, in which case reduce the cooking time to around 12 minutes.

Banana Cake

Packed with banana goodness, this is a failsafe sweet and sticky loaf cake made in a bowl with a fork and no sophistication whatsoever. The browner, mushier and generally more 'over' the bananas, the better. Don't even consider using unripe fruit.

Warm slices of banana cake can be served as a pudding with Custard (see page 33). When I last made this cake, I found two small squares of leftover cooking chocolate, cut it up with a sharp knife and poked the chunks into the raw mixture. Childish, but absolutely fantastic. You could equally add a teaspoon of ground mixed spice, a good pinch of ground cinnamon or ½ teacup of chopped walnuts or pecans.

2 medium bananas, peeled and mashed with a fork
1 egg
130g self-raising flour
1 teaspoon baking powder
55g very soft butter
100g caster sugar

Preheat the oven to 180°C/Gas Mark 4. Butter a small loaf tin, about 22 x 12cm. I line mine with baking parchment, which makes the cake easier to remove.

Put all the ingredients in a bowl and mix together, combining well with a fork. Depending on how mushy the bananas are, you might need to add a dessertspoon of warm water or milk to give the mixture a thick dropping consistency. Put the whole lot into the loaf tin and bake for 35–40 minutes. If the cake gets too brown on top, you might need to cover it loosely with a piece of foil for the last 5 minutes or so. When a fine metal skewer or a piece of raw spaghetti poked into the centre comes out clean, the cake is done. Let it cool in the tin for 5 minutes, then run a knife around the edges to loosen them and turn the cake out on to a wire rack to cool.

Alternatively, you could spoon the mixture into a muffin tray lined with paper cases, in which case reduce the cooking time to 15–20 minutes.

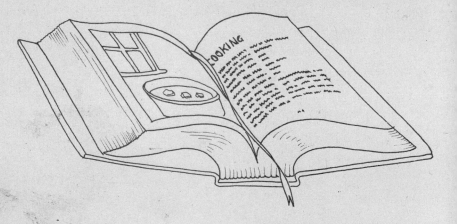

Further Inspiration

Cheese

If you have made Cottage Cheese or Paneer (see page 206) and, realising how easy it is, want to try your hand at more cheeses (it is an addictive habit once formed), you will need both good advice and starter cultures. I recommend you look at www.cheeseyogurtessentials.com.

Kitchen equipment: Fat traps

Rather than pour fat down the sink, check out www.lessmess.co.uk for more environmentally friendly ways of collecting and binning it.

Composting

I'm not going to suggest you get a chicken or pig to use up the last of your scraps – though anyone with a dog knows that they are useful for the bits left on plates. But I'll admit it: composting makes me feel good and I've only got a basic little bin from a superstore and a postage-stamp-sized garden. It's a fuss-free way to recycle organic waste and it (really) doesn't smell. If you follow some simple rules, compost is a magic gift – feeding the plants, improving the soil, controlling weeds and helping to minimise watering. And, yes, it helps reduce landfill.

Everyone knows a gardener so, even if you aren't tempted by hanging baskets or heritage seed catalogues, it's not going to be hard to find a home for all that rotted vegetable matter. All the uncooked, organic bits that simply *can't* be eaten up – the teabags, eggshells, soggy salad and banana skins – can be composted, reducing your household garbage quite substantially. Unlike landfill, well-composted food generates no methane or the nasty, polluting black slime that seeps into rivers and streams.

Basic tips:
A good compost heap needs a pretty equal amount of 'green', or nitrogen-rich, and 'brown', or carbon-rich, matter, plus air and warmth. If the balance is out of kilter, it can turn to slime and start to smell.

Start out with a layer of twiggy material, which will help to aerate the pile. Experts then advise that you should layer 'brown' and 'green' matter in roughly equal amounts, throwing in a layer of earth or manure (from a garden-centre bag kept at the side) every so often to help with the good bacteria, and sprinkling water over the pile if it looks very dry.

In reality, few of us live quite like that, but if you ensure that what you put into the bin is in roughly equal proportions of 'green' to 'brown', you will not go far wrong.

What you can compost – green:
- Garden cuttings, lawn mowings, weeds
- Dead cut flowers
- Vegetable peelings and any raw vegetables past their best
- Wilting fruit and fruit skins – but be careful not to add great heaps of acid fruit, including apples
- Used teabags, crushed eggshells, coffee grounds
- Sawdust from recently living (or 'green') wood

What you can compost – brown:
- Fallen leaves
- Shredded or scrunched-up newspaper, egg boxes, cardboard, wood ash
- Kitchen paper, so long as it is not greasy
- Small amounts of natural fibre fabrics, and (unbleached) hair
- The contents of your vacuum cleaner bag
- Dry sawdust
- Shredded office paper (not the shiny, coated kind)

What you should avoid:
- All cooked food, especially meat, as this attracts rats
- Anything non-organic (plastics, glass, tin – sounds obvious, I know)
- Animal faeces from non-vegetarian animals (i.e. no dog or cat poo)

General tips:
To help drainage and encourage worms, the bin is best placed on soil rather than a hard surface, but mine works just fine on a stone base and the worms manage to creep in through the cracks in the paving.

It is not necessary to turn the heap to encourage decomposition. If you feel like turning yours over with a garden fork every month or so, the air will encourage the bacteria to work faster, heating things up more quickly.

Victorian garden labourers were encouraged to wee into the compost to accelerate the process. It's a thought. Alternatively if you want to speed things up you can add comfrey or nettle leaves, sheep, pony, pig or chicken manure, the odd handful or two from a sack of composted farmyard manure from the local garden centre or a spade's worth from an existing pile of compost.

Most urban compost bins end up in the darkest and therefore coldest areas of the garden, which makes aesthetic sense. Bear in mind, though, that composting needs warmth, so keeping the bin in the shade will prolong the process unless you use an accelerator.

Compost is best used in the garden in spring and summer – as a top dressing or mulch (when the soil is warm and moist), or dug into the soil.

Composting meat:

Because it attracts rats and flies, adding meat to a standard compost bin is not recommended. But there are special sealed systems, known as the Green Cone and the Green Johanna, which are designed to overcome this problem and prevent vermin getting at the decomposing food. Then there's a Japanese way of composting cooked waste including meat, known as the Bokashi bucket system – two buckets made of a special plastic with impregnated Effective Micro-Organisms (EMs), which both begin the breaking-down process and counteract smell. Waste food is then layered with a special bran, also treated with EMs. When the bucket is full, it's left for 10 to 14 days, after which you can add the contents to your compost pile. Meanwhile, you get on with using the second bucket.

None of these systems comes cheap, at around £50 for a Green Cone, £75 for a Green Johanna and upwards of £80 for the biggest two-bucket Bokashi set. It's worth checking to see if your local council will provide them on a non-profit basis.

Further information:
- The Organic Gardening Catalogue (www.organiccatalog.com) can supply two wooden bins that slot together.
- Modular composters, wormeries, Green Cones, Green Johannas and Bokashi buckets are also available from www.wigglywigglers.co.uk and www.greencone.com.
- Most garden centres supply basic plastic composters.

Index

celeriac: beef hash 155
    and potato mash 97, 152
    soups 56, 58
celery: chicken pie 94
    gratin 99–100
    Italian beef salad 214
    roast 103, 221
    in soups 56, 60, 62, 64
chard, rustic fried 157
cheese 90, 190
    Arancini 140
    bakes 90
    bubble and squeak 152
    cauliflower cheese 98
    in fishcakes 143
    gratins 98–100
    home-made 190, 205–6
    macaroni cheese 99
    melted 202
    muffins 241, 243
    omelette 191
    in pies 117, 118, 119
    pizza 128
    potato cakes 135
    risotto 179
    salad: pulses and nuts 216
        roast vegetable 211
    sauce 31, 32
    savoury pancakes 198
    soufflé 203, 204
    Spanish omelette 194, 195
    straws 113
    tarts 121, 122
    on toast 201–2
    see also individual types
chicken 26
    Arabic bake (fatta) 101
    fricassée 160–61
    fried rice 175
    jambalaya 179–80
    marinades 38
    meatballs 144–5
        in broth 67
    pasta bakes 185
    pie: filo 124
        pastry 114–15
        potato-topped 94–5
    pilaf 172, 173
    pizza 128
    puttanesca 74
    risotto 178, 179
    salads: Gado gado 212
        pulses 217
        roast vegetable 210, 211
    savoury pancakes 198
    soups 64–5
    Spanish omelette 194
    stews 72–4, 75
    stir-fries 164, 166
    stroganoff 159
    Thai curry 86–7

chickpeas: in chicken stew 74
    salads 216, 217
    in soups 60–3, 65
    spinach and 146
    in yogurt sauce 77
chicory: gratin 99
    potato salad 218
    Trinxat 153
chilli jam 39, 45
chocolate 223, 246
chorizo: in chicken stew 74
    and chickpea salad 217
    Jambalaya 179
    refreshed pasta with 183
    Ribollita 61
    rustic fried green vegetables 157
    Spanish omelette 194
Christmas leftovers: hash 155
    Jambalaya 179
    meatballs 146
    omelette 192
    pasta 185
    pie 116
    potted turkey 211
    soup 65
    vegetables, fried green 157
chutney 39
    apple 42
    tomato 43
cottage cheese 205, 206
    salad 208, 211
cottage pie 96–7
courgettes 27
    and cheese tart 122
    in curry 88
    minestrone 62–3
    muffins 243
    in ragù 79
    ratatouille 80–81
    roast 103
    soufflé 205
    Spanakopita 123–4, 187
    Spanish omelette 194–5
    stuffed 147–8
    vegetable salad 209
    in yogurt sauce 77
cream 19, 21
croûtons 52, 55
crumble, fruit 236–7
curry 70, 82–8, 205
    hot Indian 84–5
    meatballs 147
    mild Indian 82–3
    Thai 86–8
custard 31, 33
    baked 33, 245

dips 19, 39
    aubergine 48
    guacamole 48
dressings 208, 209, 210–11

duck: fat 31
    salad dressing for 210
    shredded: roast duck pie 116
        with vegetable salad 210

eggs 19
    eggs Benedict 31
    eggy bread 221
    omelettes 190–5
    poached: buck rabbit 201
    scrambled 192
    soufflé 203–5
        cheese 204
    whites, freezing 22, 33, 199
        meringues 199
    yolks, freezing 22, 199
        custard 31, 33
        zabaglione 200
endive and blue cheese: pie 119
    tart 122

fennel: and black pudding tart 121
    in chicken fricassée 160
    fish bake 93
    in pies 114, 117
    in pilaf 173
    Ribollita 61
    in risotto 178
    rustic fried 157
    salads 211, 214, 218
    Spanish omelette 194
    tart 122
feta: in filo pie 123–5
    in potato cakes 135
    pumpkin and leek tart 121
    with roast vegetables 102–3
        salad 211
    in Spanish omelette 195
filo pastry 113
    meatball mixture in 148
    pies 123–5
        cheese 118–19
        poultry, Middle Eastern 116
        Spanakopita 123–4
        Tunisian meat 118
fish 19, 24, 26
    bakes 93
    broth 67
    curry 82, 87
    fishcakes 134, 142–3
    kedgeree 171
    marinades 37–8
    omelette 192
    pie 91–3
        making into soup 68
        smoked fish 92
        white fish 118
    pilaf 174
    poached 142
    risotto 176, 178
    salad dressing for 210, 211

Acknowledgements

Most of my recipes have been accumulated over so many years that things I cooked first at university, when I started work, for new (now old) friends, when I was travelling round the world or when I began to make a home are all jumbled up together. Reading back through them is almost better than a diary. The pages are full of the memories of people, places, sights, smells and – particularly – things tried or tasted for the first time. All decorated with a load of gravy, egg and flour. I've never thrown food away – my mother's daughter – so this really is the way that I cook.

All cooking requires a magpie mind, so thanks are due to everyone with whom I've ever shared food, but for some of the ideas in this book, I must thank particularly: Manoj Vasaikar at Indian Zing, Rosie Glazebrook, Caroline Muirhead, Jane Brashish Ellames, Ken Cox, Lucinda Coulthard, Ashutosh Khandekar, Anissa Helou, Lila das Gupta, Emily and Ned Campbell, Pino at La Picola, Hammersmith, Emily Sweet, Christine Smith.

Thanks to Caroline Dawnay at United Agents, to Richard Atkinson, Jane Middleton and Natalie Hunt at Bloomsbury, and to Will Webb for his fantastic design and illustrations.

For growing so much of the food I've ever eaten, thank you Dad. And for being a better cook than me, thanks mum. Our kids, Freddie and Bill, deserve a medal for putting up with endless amounts of banana cake and my husband, David Miller, is, was and always shall be, the true god of the wok.